W9-CKI-986

★★★★★★THE ★★★★★NEW CONGRESS

Change has been a constant factor in the history of the Congress of the United States. No period has been marked by as great a change as the last decade. This book traces the unique qualities that have historically marked both houses and brought them to a time of crisis. Recently some changes of a basic nature have enabled Congress to reassume a coequal role in the national government, challenging the presidency in matters of war powers, impeachment, and the basic substance of government responsibility.

by STEPHEN GOODE

Published by Julian Messner, a Simon & Schuster
Division of Gulf & Western Corporation,
Simon & Schuster Building,
1230 Avenue of the Americas,
New York, New York 10020.
Second Printing, 1981
JULIAN MESSNER and colophon are trademarks of
Simon & Schuster, registered in the U.S. Patent
and Trademark Office.
Manufactured in the United States of America.
Design by Irving Perkins
Library of Congress Cataloging in Publication Data
Goode, Stephen.
The new Congress.
Bibliography: p.
Includes index.
SUMMARY: Provides historical background for and
describes the problems that led to the reforms and
changes that have taken place in Congress in the 1970's.
1. United States. Congress—Juvenile literature.
[1. United States. Congress] I. Title.
JK1051.G66 328.73 80-19111
ISBN 0-671-34031-X

For Harold Poor and Tom Kersch

CONTENTS

Chapter One:	The Congress of the United States	9
Chapter Two:	Congress and the Constitution	31
Chapter Three:	The House in Practice	50
Chapter Four:	The Senate in Practice	74
Chapter Five:	Congress in Crisis	97
Chapter Six:	Preliminary Steps Toward Reform	121
Chapter Seven:	Congress Reforms Itself	142
Chapter Eight:	Congress Challenges a President	164
Chapter Nine:	Congress and the Watergate Affair	183
Chapter Ten:	Problems	200
	Suggestions for Further Reading	207
	Index	213

CHAPTER ONE

THE CONGRESS OF THE UNITED STATES

The cares of politics engross a prominent place in the occupations of a citizen in the United States; and almost the only pleasure which an American knows is to take a part in the government, and to discuss its measures—Alexis de Tocqueville, DEMOCRACY IN AMERICA

I

WHEN THE French aristocrat and political scientist, Alexis de Tocqueville, wrote the passage quoted above after his visit to the United States in 1831 and 1832, he referred to the unusual interest Americans took in all levels of political life, from the local town meeting to the highest levels of the federal government. In America, he continued, "even the women frequently attend public meetings, and listen to political harangues as a recreation from their household labors." If the average American were forced to end his fascination with politics, de Tocqueville concluded, "he would be robbed of one half of his existence; he would feel an immense void in the life which he is accustomed to lead, and his wretchedness would be unbearable."

Although a century and a half have passed since de Tocqueville observed America, his words still hold true. Americans now pursue many pleasures, but remain engrossed and captivated by the political life of the nation. Some observers have noticed a disenchantment with politics among some Americans and a feeling that "politics makes no difference," but this disenchantment is not widespread. Every election year, the news media devote an enormous amount of time and energy to covering the candidates and their issues. Contenders for political office from the President down to the local mayor or sheriff are closely scrutinized and observed, while the public follows national campaigns with an interest usually directed toward film stars or sports events.

Much of the attention Americans give to politics is focused on the Congress of the United States. This should not be surprising. The Founding Fathers, who drew up the Constitution almost two hundred years ago, intended that the Congress would express the "voice of the people" and bring the influence of that voice to bear on national policy. In the words of James Madison, later the fourth President of the United States, they hoped that representative government would "refine and enlarge the public views by passing them through the medium of a chosen body of citizens," elected by the people to Congress because they were wiser, more talented, and better able to articulate the needs of the country than was the average citizen.

The Congress envisioned by the Founding Fathers was a place where the pulse of the nation could be felt directly and where the public would find its complaints, desires, and wants expressed and redressed. Such a Congress, the Founding Fathers realized, could not work isolated from the public view. It could function and thrive only when the people maintained the deep and lively interest in political life described by de Tocqueville—the interest the public still shows today, in spite of the increased complexities of modern life.

Public attention is drawn to Congress because what the members of Congress say and do affects the lives of every American citizen. The Constitution grants Congress "all legislative powers" possessed by the federal government. These powers include the right to set taxes and to decide how tax money is to be spent. They include the power to declare war, to ratify or reject treaties with foreign nations, to confirm or dismiss presidential appointments to public office, to conduct investigations into the affairs and activities of government officials, and many other powers important to the well-being of the nation. A strong Congress, conscious of its constitutional prerogatives and willing to exercise its powers, is fully equal to the President and can significantly influence the national destiny. But even a weak Congress—and there have been several in the history of the United States—can make its will felt and on occasion restrain the actions of a strong chief executive.

Many constitutional scholars agree that aside from its right to declare war the most extraordinary power possessed by Congress is its "power of the purse." This power—the power to tax and to spend—gives the Congress the ability to set national goals and establish priorities. A defense-minded Congress, for instance, can choose to emphasize military and related spending programs at the expense of other national interests, whereas a Congress of a different mind can choose to emphasize the need for spending in the field of human services, such as welfare, health and medical programs, and public education. In either case, the manner in which Congress decides to spend federal money will help determine the course and development of American society for many years to come.

Another power granted the Congress by the Constitution is the right "to regulate commerce with foreign nations, and among the several states. . . ." Until 1887, this power was little exercised. But since that time, Congress has passed legislation regulating many areas of financial and business life. Trusts and monopolies have been outlawed, and various laws have been enacted that control the interstate transportation of explosives, narcotics, prostitutes, and foods or drugs that are mislabeled or of questionable quality. Critics of extensive congressional power claim that these regulations unnecessarily restrict the business life of the nation. Supporters, on the other hand, point out that Congress has the duty to protect the public from exploitation and from materials dangerous to the health and welfare of the country.

The power to ratify or reject treaties gives the Congress an important influence in the making of foreign policy. Its right to confirm or dismiss presidential appointments allows Congress to have a say as to who will sit in the President's cabinet or hold other high public offices. On occasion, an angry Congress has destroyed international plans and proposals carefully developed and supported by a President. This was the case after World War I, when Woodrow Wilson's hopes for American participation in the League of Nations were repudiated by a Congress tired of war and of American participation in the affairs of other nations. In other instances, however, the Congress has chosen to work closely with the President and support his policies, as when Republicans and Democrats united in a bipartisan effort behind Harry Truman during the early years of the cold war.

Since 1789, Congress has rejected only eight presidential appointments to cabinet-level posts after careful screenings that exposed the lives and characters of these appointees to public view. Other presidential appointments, however, have not fared so well. Roughly one in five nominations to the Supreme Court has been dismissed, often in a highly dramatic fashion that showed that Congress could challenge the chief executive and successfully overcome his wishes. During his first administration, President Nixon experienced two successive rejections of men he had appointed to the high court: Clement Haynsworth, Jr., and G. Harrold Carswell. President Nixon deeply resented the rejections and believed his authority had been unjustly attacked. But for the members of Congress who had voted against the appointments, the rejections were merely an assertion of the congressional duty to deny office to men they considered to be of questionable character or mediocre ability.

In recent years, one of the most striking powers exercised by Congress has been its right to investigate the activities and affairs of government officials. Congressional investigations have played an important part in American history since the early years of Congress. But the widespread use of television and other media coverage in the past three decades has made these investigations more conspicuous and visible to the public eye.

Congressional investigations have led to the enactment of new laws that redress old grievances and to changes in government policies that have proved mistaken or wrongheaded. Investigations have also resulted in the downfall of prominent politicians. During the late 1960s, for instance, the Fulbright committee's investigations into the reasons for American participation in the Vietnam War helped to convince many members of Congress who had earlier supported the war that the American involvement should be brought to an end. In 1973 and 1974, when two other congressional committees looked into the activities of President Nixon and his assistants, their work led to the resignation of many of the President's most trusted advisers and finally to the resignation of the President himself, under charges of misconduct while in office.

The powers Congress exercises—its power of the purse, its ability to influence foreign policy, its right to confirm presidential appointments, and its various other powers—make the Capitol, where Congress meets, one of the important centers of American political life. Every year, the members of Congress receive thousands of letters from constituents who seek favors or ask that their elected official take a certain stand on political issues of the day. Sometimes these requests come from elderly citizens concerned about their Social Security payments. At other times, they come from men and women deeply involved with controversial problems such as abortion, women's rights, or taxation.

But Congress not only draws the attention of private citizens throughout the country. It is also closely watched by interest groups and organizations centered in Washington, whose purpose is to keep close tabs on Congress and to influence individual members of Congress to support legislation that will benefit their groups. Every major American corporation is represented by a team of men and women, called lobbyists, and there are lobbyists who work for the nation's banking interests, private insurance companies, and a host of other businesses and commercial enterprises.

On occasion, critics of Washington politics have complained that these lobbies possess too much power and wealth and are able to dominate and control Congress in a way impossible for the average citizen, whose resources are limited. Congress has responded to these criticisms by passing laws designed to restrict lobbying activities and make it illegal to buy support from members of Congress with gifts or money. In addition to the lobbies representing private financial interests, there are lobbies that act for the interests and concerns of fundamentalist Christians, labor unions, consumers, supporters of women's rights, and numerous other elements of American society.

II

CONGRESS, HOWEVER, is more than the powers it wields, as impressive as these may be. It is more than its ability to tax and spend, conduct investigations, ratify treaties, or declare war. From the time the first House and Senate met in 1789, Congress has been the visible embodiment of the values and character of the American people. On occasion, it has reflected the best of these values: the American concern for the underdog, the love of individual freedom and fair play, and the struggle for equality. But at other times, it has done little more than mirror the selfishness and aggression, the greed and petty concerns that are a part of everyone.

One reason Congress reflects the values of the nation is that individual members of Congress come to stand for, or symbolize, important political traditions and movements. During the first half of the nineteenth century, for instance, Henry Clay (Whig, Kentucky), Daniel Webster (Whig, Massachusetts), and John C. Calhoun (Democrat, South Carolina) were men much admired by the people of the country. Frequently, their fame eclipsed that of the Presidents of the time. Clay, whose brilliant political skills enabled him to unite political opponents in meaningful compromise, was an advocate of early American nationalism and what he called "the American system." Webster, the greatest orator in Senate history, represented the interests and traditions of New England, whereas Calhoun, the most original political philosopher America has produced, looked after the concerns of his native South.

In our own century, men of comparable caliber and stature have served in Congress. These have included Robert La Follette (Progressive Republican, Wisconsin), Robert Taft (Republican, Ohio), Richard Russell (Democrat, Georgia), Hubert Humphrey (Democrat, Minnesota), and Robert Kennedy (Democrat, New York). Taft and Russell were outstanding conservatives; La Follette, Humphrey, and Kennedy were advocates of liberal and progressive values. Our own century too has seen the addition of women to the ranks of Congress, among whom Margaret Chase Smith (Republican, Maine) has been prominent and widely respected.

Reputations earned in Congress have led twenty-two men on to the office of President. From the House of Representatives came

James Madison, Abraham Lincoln, and James Polk, as well as Rutherford B. Hayes, James Garfield, William McKinley, and Gerald Ford. James Monroe, John Quincy Adams, Harry Truman, Martin Van Buren, John Tyler, and Benjamin Harrison served with distinction in the Senate. Others, including Richard Nixon, Lyndon Johnson, John Kennedy, and Andrew Jackson, had careers in both houses of Congress.

On occasion, individual acts of courage by members of Congress have raised them from the ranks of politicians merely adept at "getting along" to the status of statesmen concerned about the interests of the nation as a whole. In 1847, for instance, Abraham Lincoln (Whig, Illinois), against the best political advice he could receive, made a speech before the House of Representatives in which he called for an end to slavery in the District of Columbia, a topic almost completely avoided by his fellow representatives. But Lincoln was an advocate of lost causes. The next year, he lost his bid for reelection to the House because he spoke out against America's participation in the Mexican War.

Fortunately, Lincoln has not stood alone. His act of courage has been matched by other similar acts on the part of men and women such as Thomas B. Reed (Republican, Maine), Margaret Chase Smith, Hubert Humphrey, Wayne Morse (Democrat, Oregon), and Ernest Gruening (Democrat, Alaska). At the height of the war fever against Spain in the late 1890s, Reed, a powerful member of the House of Representatives, opposed the war, which was loudly supported by his own political party. He likewise opposed the acquisition of colonies by the United States, claiming that the subjugation of foreign peoples by America was against the American traditions of independence and freedom.

Margaret Chase Smith and Hubert Humphrey are now highly regarded for controversial positions they took in the 1950s. Almost alone in Congress, Humphrey strongly and vociferously defended civil rights for black Americans and demanded that

America right the wrongs it had committed against that race at a time when most senators and representatives wanted to move slowly in that direction, if at all. Margaret Smith, independent and strong-willed, was one of the few senators to recognize Senator Joseph McCarthy's anticommunist campaign for the charade it had become and to have the courage to denounce McCarthy's questionable tactics and behavior. Morse and Gruening are remembered because out of the one hundred members of the Senate, they were the only two to oppose America's commitment to the Vietnam War at the time of the Tonkin Gulf Resolution.

Unluckily, however, for every prominent and highly regarded member of Congress, there have been others perceived by the public as dishonest, corrupt, and crooked. On several occasions, Washington has been rocked by scandals involving congressmen, scandals that sometimes reached near epidemic proportions and reflected on every elected official in the capital, innocent as well as guilty. This was true in the early 1870s in the case of Oakes Dawes (Republican, Massachusetts).

In addition to serving as a member of the House of Representatives, Dawes also happened to be a stockholder in Union Pacific, a railroad company that sought favorable legislation from Congress. In order to sway congressional opinion toward approval of Union Pacific's interests, Dawes distributed stock in a construction company called the Credit Mobilier as gifts to several of his fellow representatives. The Credit Mobilier had been organized by Union Pacific and was subject to its wishes. Its purpose was to divert profits from railroad construction to a few select promoters, while Union Pacific itself appeared to be on the verge of bankruptcy.

When word of the transaction reached the public, newspaper editors and others demanded that Dawes and his accomplices be punished. In the election year 1872, the House of Representatives, whose members were concerned that public indignation might cause them to lose their elected offices, voted 182 to 36 to "condemn" Dawes. No other action, however, was taken against Dawes or against those members of Congress who had benefited from his largesse. To many Americans, the failure of Congress to act against this type of corruption seemed to be proof that congressmen were bound by no responsibility except to their own private concerns and interests and could easily use their office for personal gain and enrichment.

More recent outbreaks of scandal occurred in the 1970s. Within a short period of time, two powerful members of Congress, Wilbur Mills (Democrat, Arkansas) and Wayne Hays (Democrat, Ohio) made national headlines in separate incidents that cast doubt on the personal morality and life-styles of officials throughout the capital. Their cases gained rapid notoriety because both men headed important committees in the House of Representatives. Mills was Chairman of the Ways and Means Committee and was regarded as an expert on taxation and government spending. Hays chaired the House Administration Committee.

Mills's downfall began late one night when his car was stopped for a traffic violation not far from the Washington Monument. At first, Mills attempted to impress the policeman with his position in Congress, but a passenger in his car, Fanny Foxe, a local dancer and entertainer, panicked and ran, jumping from the street into the Tidal Basin. The next day, all of Washington discussed the incident. In the disclosures that followed, it was found that Mills, who had always impressed those who knew him as a sober, serious, and hardworking congressman, had struggled for some time with alcoholism. He was said to have frequented nightclubs and to have spent lavishly on drink and entertainment.

Mills's fall from power was quick and decisive. He lost his important seat on the Ways and Means Committee and eventually left the House of Representatives where he had served many years with great distinction. Subsequently, Mills overcame his alcoholism, but the damage to his career and to the reputation of Congress had already been done.

The case of Wayne Hays was equally bizarre. His downfall began one Sunday morning when the *Washington Post* carried a carefully researched story about Elizabeth Ray, a woman who worked in Hays's congressional office. Ray, who cooperated with the *Post* in bringing the story to light, confessed that she had been hired as Hays's companion and mistress. She further claimed that she had no secretarial skills; she could take no dictation and could not operate a typewriter. Her presence in Hays's office served no useful purpose, yet she was kept on the House payroll at an unusually high salary for a person of her qualifications.

The revelations were all the more striking because Hays, who was regarded as a tyrant by many of his fellow representatives, had made a name for himself as a no-nonsense representative, concerned about waste and extravagance. Like Mills, Wayne Hays lost his committee chairmanship and his seat in Congress.* But the two cases have lingered in the public mind and have helped to sustain the image many Americans have of Congress as a place where seriousness and hard work are rare.

Because of the prominent place it plays in the life of the nation, Congress has often felt the sting of the great American humorists and satirists. In the last decades of the nineteenth century, Mark Twain mercilessly lambasted the smugness and pomposity he believed characterized the legislators of his time—the period that saw the Oakes Dawes scandal and others. "It could probably be shown by facts and figures," Twain wrote, "that there is no distinctly native American criminal class except Congress."

* Hays, an able politician, now serves his home district in the Ohio state legislature.

On another occasion, when he discovered thieves who had broken into his home, the story was told that Twain had lectured them severely and had warned the burglars that if they didn't change their illegal habits, they would "end up in the United States Senate." But Twain reserved his harshest criticism of his time for his novel *The Gilded Age: A Tale of Today* (1873), which he wrote in collaboration with Charles Dudley Warner. Rarely has an American author presented a more shocking picture of government corruption. In Twain's view, the nation had sunk so low that scoundrels and other worthless types now controlled Congress. When the friend of Colonel Sanders, one of his characters, suggests that the colonel should consider running for the Senate or the House, the colonel is deeply offended. "I don't think," he replies to his friend, "there has ever been anything in my conduct that should make you feel justified in saying a thing like that." Clearly, Twain's colonel believed himself to be several cuts above the sort of man who could abide the corruption and dishonesty of congressional life.

In this century, two other figures, H. L. Mencken and Will Rogers, continued the tradition begun by Mark Twain. Mencken, a journalist who lived in Baltimore, loved to cover the political scene. "Going into politics," he wrote, "is fatal to a gentleman." Mencken found politics to be "a carnival of buncombe" * and "a clown show." He was endlessly fascinated by what he found to be the lack of imagination and stupidity of the politicians of his time. He recognized the at best mediocre talents of most of them

* Mencken took the word *buncombe* from a speech made in Congress by a representative from Buncombe County, North Carolina. The speech, which was made to please the representative's constituents and gain their approval, was full of nonsense and hot air. The speaker, however, excused himself by saying that he was "speaking for Buncombe." Hence *buncombe* or *bunk* has come to stand for any form of insincere talk, humbug, or claptrap.

and took joy in puncturing their pretentions to greatness and their feelings of self-importance.

Will Rogers's satiric barbs directed at Washington were probably heard by a larger audience than either Mark Twain's or H. L. Mencken's. A popular radio personality, he also appeared on the stage and in movies. Rogers styled himself as a simple cowboy from Oklahoma, but he was actually a sophisticated performer and a man of unusual insight and common sense. Our "Congress is the best money can buy," he said, in an ironic allusion not to congressional salaries but to the bribes many members of Congress were known to have taken from wealthy financial interests. "I just watch the government and report the facts," Rogers declared, and keep a close watch on all those people we elect to "misrun" Congress.

Rogers was of the opinion that "politics ain't on the level" and that the government did its best governing during the summer months when all the bureaucrats and officials left the capital city to escape the heat. But what frequently bothered him the most about Congress was not the corruption some senators and representatives succumbed to; corruption and dishonesty, he knew, could be expected to spring up wherever human beings worked together. Rogers, like many other Americans of his time, was more deeply disturbed by the inability of Congress to come to a final decision about important issues during a time of national crisis.

During the early years of the Great Depression of the 1930s, when millions were out of work and hungry, the House of Representatives and the Senate could not agree on any program to relieve the misery the depression had caused. "I don't think we have anybody in Washington that don't want to feed 'em," Rogers said, "but they all want to feed 'em their way." Democracy is a luxury we all enjoy, he seemed to be saying, but when our elected officials indulge in unlimited discussion without getting anything done, then the people have a right to be dissatisfied.

III

SINCE THE time the first House of Representatives and Senate assembled in 1789 in New York City, then the capital of the United States, Congress has undergone many changes. One of the most striking of these changes has been in the character and makeup of its membership. The present Congress, for instance, possesses a degree of professionalism and ability unusual in American history. Present-day members of Congress are generally well educated, knowledgeable about domestic and world affairs, and served by staffs of aides and assistants of high caliber and dedication.

This has not always been the case. In the nineteenth century, Congress, and especially the House of Representatives, was characterized by a roughness and vulgarity that often shocked foreign visitors to the United States. It was a time when the brilliant but erratic John Randolph of Virginia, a Jeffersonian Democrat, could have his hunting dogs beside him when he spoke from the floor of the House and when spittoons, for spitting tobacco juice, were in abundance in both chambers of Congress. It was a time too when many representatives were almost illiterate, like the great folk hero, Davy Crockett (Democrat, Tennessee).

Fantastic stories about the behavior of the congressmen of this time abound. Fights often broke out in Congress and sometimes political disagreements were settled by duels that ended in bloodshed or death. On one occasion, Senator Henry "Hangman" Foote (Democrat, Mississippi) drew a pistol in the Senate against Senator Thomas Hart Benton * (Democrat, Missouri), who was saved

* Senator Benton was known for his ability to use pistols. Years earlier he had received a wound in a street brawl with Andrew Jackson, later a President of the United States.

only by the intervention of other senators. In 1856, Senator Charles Sumner (Republican, Massachusetts), a strong opponent of slavery, was beaten almost to death by two representatives from South Carolina, as he sat at his Senate desk. Other senators watched, but did not come to his aid. It took Sumner two years to recover from the attack, but his assailants were never punished. They returned to the South, where they were regarded as heroes.

Other changes have also taken place in Congress. In the early years of congressional history, the House of Representatives was generally regarded as the more powerful and influential of the two divisions of Congress. This favored position resulted largely from the work of two House leaders, James Madison and later Henry Clay, whose legislative abilities surpassed those of any senator of the time. By 1830, however, the Senate had emerged as the center for the discussion of the great national issues that arose as the Civil War approached, a position the Senate has maintained in the public eye to this day.

The House of Representatives has never accepted this change of status, and over the years its relationship with the Senate has been marked by frequent jurisdictional disputes and petty jealousies. These disputes led John Nance Garner (Democrat, Texas), a powerful Speaker of the House, to defend the institution he belonged to. "The House of Representatives," Garner told a listener, "is not the 'lower' house. It is the most numerous, but not the 'lower.' In the most important functions of taxes, appropriations, and control of the purse, it is the originating and, therefore, the highest house."

Garner's description of the House as the "most numerous" branch of Congress points to the chief difference between the two bodies: size. The first House of Representatives had fifty-nine members, whereas the first Senate had only twenty-six. By 1890, the House had grown to 357 and twenty years later, in 1910, it had 435 members, the number it has maintained to the present day, in spite of the enormous increase in America's population. The Senate, by comparison, today has 100 members, or 335 fewer than the House.

This striking disparity in size has played an important part in the development and evolution of each body. Because of its rapid growth and large membership, the House has had to curtail the individuality and independence of its members in order that its business can be carried out and completed. It has imposed on its 435 members a large body of rules so that their day-to-day work will not dissolve into chaos and disorder. The smaller Senate, on the other hand, is relatively free of rules and regulations, a fact that allows it to conduct its business in a more leisurely fashion.

The smaller size of the Senate has meant that a larger number of senators can enjoy national fame and prominence, since there are fewer of them to know and recognize, whereas representatives must endure relative anonymity. It has also meant that senators can be allowed almost unlimited debate and discussion on issues before their chamber compared with the strict time limits that must be placed on members of the other house. The right of debate and discussion is a jealously guarded privilege of the Senate, a privilege envied by many representatives who look forward to the time when they will have the chance to run for election to the "upper" house.

The way power and authority have been exercised in the House and Senate has changed from time to time over the years. There have been periods when strong Speakers, like Thomas B. Reed and Joseph Cannon (Republican, Illinois), could control the House and have it carry out their wishes. Similarly, the Senate has been dominated by powerful majority leaders such as Lyndon Johnson (Democrat, Texas), who seemed to stand head and shoulders above the other senators of their time.

But there have been other periods of congressional history

when power and influence were held by the chairmen of important committees or by other small groups of senators and representatives. These men (women have yet to play a significant role in the inner circles of congressional power) ruled the House of Representatives and the Senate by the sheer power of their legislative ability and by the authority and respect they had accumulated. The practice of seniority, by which members of Congress who have served the longest received the most coveted committee chairmanships, helped these figures acquire the authority they exercised. Through the seniority system, by getting reelected frequently enough, a representative or senator of even mediocre ability could hope eventually to play an influential role in congressional affairs, while a man of superior skills could become one of the significant forces in Washington.

The history of Congress is the story of the constant tilt between the power of tradition and the power of change and innovation. When tradition is strong, the House and Senate seem bound by patterns of behavior and rules of procedure they have followed for decades. Tradition provides much needed order and regularity in the unusually chaotic practice of American politics, but it provides this order and regularity at a price. The Congresses of the 1950s and early 1960s, for instance, were regarded by many as out of touch with the needs and concerns of the nation. Congressional business was carried on as usual during this period; new, important laws were passed and investigations conducted, but the overall picture conveyed by Congress was that of an institution ingrained in and limited by its own traditions.

Other periods of congressional history, on the other hand, have been marked by change and a rebellious attitude toward tradition and the status quo. These periods have been more frequent and dramatic in the House of Representatives, where the weight of tradition and regulation sits more heavily on individual members than in the Senate, with its relatively greater amount of freedom. But change and reform have come from time to time to both chambers.

Changes in the life of Congress usually reflect changes that have already taken place in the life of the nation. This is true of the two periods of significant change and innovation that have taken place in Congress in this century. During the first, which centered around the years 1910 and 1913, rebellious members of the House of Representatives stripped Speaker Joe Cannon of his powers, which many regarded as dictatorial and tyrannical, and turned many of the powers once held by the House leader over to the chairmen of the principal committees.

Further reform—this time by the Seventeenth Amendment to the Constitution—resulted in the direct election of senators by the people of the states rather than by the state legislatures, as the Constitution had originally provided. Both reforms, the fall of Speaker Cannon and the direct election of senators, came at a time when the nation had long demanded change. Progressive movements had rocked both the Democratic and Republican parties. Everywhere, the call was to throw the old guard out and establish greater democracy and efficiency in government institutions. It was the era of American history that began with the attacks on trusts and monopolies, ran through President Theodore Roosevelt's crusades for reform, and ended with President Wilson and his program of a "new freedom" for America.

The second period of significant congressional reform in this century, which reached its peak between 1970 and 1976, followed a similar time of social ferment and discontent. Once again, the call was for greater democracy and greater government efficiency in handling human needs and complaints. Beginning with the civil rights movement, the 1960s witnessed the birth of a number of causes—including women's rights, environmentalism, consumerism, the antiwar movement, and others—that undermined public complacency and challenged the status quo.

Eventually, this spirit of reform took hold of Congress, as it had taken hold of much of the nation. Major civil rights legislation was passed in 1964, and gradually the political makeup of the House and Senate changed from conservative to liberal. Many members of Congress began to question America's participation in the Vietnam War and to call for a reassessment of America's role in world affairs. Concern and interest were likewise expressed for improvement of the nation's policies in dealing with natural resources, the pollution of air, water, and landscape, and the needs of America's many minorities.

By the early 1970s, the stage was set for a meaningful reform of Congress itself. A new generation of senators and representatives had filled many seats in Congress that had been vacated by older, often more conservative members. And this new generation was characterized by a lack of allegiance to the old ways of doing business and by a belief that Congress, as it was now constituted, was too restrictive and limiting. Fresh air was needed, they believed, and a better way of conducting business, one that allowed for more innovation and experimentation.

The new generation of senators and representatives united its efforts with an older generation of liberals and congressional mavericks * who had long hoped for change and reform. The result was electric. In a short time, the seniority system had been called into question and several well-known and prominent committee chairmen had lost their power. Alterations were made in many House and Senate rules, and the force of tradition lost much

* A congressional maverick is a senator or representative who is known for his or her independence. A maverick votes the party line only occasionally and cannot be identified with any ideological or interest group in Congress.

of its authority. The "new Congress"—the subject of this book—that emerged from these reforms was marked by a vitality and sense of mission that have been rare in congressional history.

The reforms that characterized the new Congress reflected many of the concerns of the liberal and radical movements of the 1960s. The new Congress wanted greater openness in government and less secrecy and back-door maneuvering. It wanted power and influence to be shared by a large number of senators and representatives, rather than exercised by a small number of congressional leaders and powerful committee chairmen. The new Congress, in short, hoped to make the House and Senate more democratic by making the legislative process visible to all Americans and by allotting decision-making responsibility to as many senators and representatives as possible.

But there was one more reform the new Congress wanted to make, and this reform brought it into direct confrontation with the President of the United States. For almost forty years, since the time of President Franklin Roosevelt, who took office in 1933, the powers and influence of the presidency had steadily increased while the power and prestige of Congress decreased. More and more, the public came to look to the President for leadership and guidance and to view the Congress as, at best, a secondary branch of government.

The reasons for this phenomenon are not difficult to determine. From the 1930s to the present day, the United States has faced a series of crises, beginning with the Great Depression and followed by World War II and the cold war. During this period, the President was the one public figure who could provide the unified leadership and direction the country needed in order to survive. When Congress submitted to presidential authority, it did so not so much out of weakness as out of concern that anything that might hamper the chief executive's ability to act quickly might play into the hands of our enemies.

The result was an erosion of the constitutional ideal of a balance of power among the three branches of the federal government: the legislative, the executive, and judicial. Under Roosevelt and the Presidents who followed, legislative programs became the responsibility of the President and his growing body of advisers, who drew them up and then submitted them to Congress for approval. This was not unprecedented. Strong Presidents, like Lincoln, Theodore Roosevelt, and Wilson, had exerted powerful influence on Congress to pass the legislation they sought. What was new under Franklin Roosevelt and afterward was the degree to which Congress lost the initiative in foreign affairs and domestic policy. Nothing new now seemed to originate in the House or Senate. Instead, when the Congress challenged the chief executive, it did so in a negative fashion by delaying or watering down controversial bills, by debating fine points of presidential budgets, or by strongly criticizing executive actions without offering alternative programs.

This was the state of affairs that confronted the new congresses of the 1970s and that they wanted to change. Gone were the days when the Congress played a role inferior to that of the President. The new House and Senate demanded a part in government equal to that of the executive branch, as the Constitution had planned. This meant that Congress would have to originate new legislative programs on its own, plan budgets by its own expertise, and offer useful alternatives to actions carried out by the President.

The creation of a more active Congress also meant that the power and authority of the President would have to be confronted and confronted directly. Without a check on executive authority, the increased power and vitality of Congress might accomplish little. The confrontation developed in two ways. On the one hand, bills were passed over presidential veto. Some of these bills, such as the War Powers Act, were designed to restrict the powers exercised by the President. On the other hand, the House and

Senate made use of their right of investigation to look into the activities of one controversial and strong President, Richard Nixon, and to uncover a series of criminal acts committed by Nixon and his staff. This discovery sent several staff members to jail and forced the resignation of the President.

This book will look into the origins and character of this new Congress that reformed itself and challenged the power of the President. But first we shall look at the Constitution, discuss the powers it grants to Congress, and make a brief historical survey of the evolution and development of the House and Senate. An understanding of congressional history will help us understand the significance of the recent reforms. This will be followed by a description of the problems that made the changes of the 1970s, in the view of many Washington observers, necessary and long overdue. In the last half of the book, we shall look at the nature and character of the reforms themselves and decide whether they did indeed succeed in creating a "new Congress."

One final note before we begin. Some experts have judged the reforms of the 1970s to be the most sweeping changes Congress has ever experienced. Others have been less sanguine, complaining that the reforms did not go far enough or that they left basic problems untouched. Whatever our conclusion, however, we must be impressed by the ability of a body like Congress to criticize its own activities and attempt reform. No government can be perfect, but one that can allow for a certain amount of change from time to time can likewise hope for the correction of past mistakes and be able to make improvements based on its own experience.

CHAPTER TWO

CONGRESS AND THE CONSTITUTION

All legislative Powers herein granted shall be vested in a Congress of the United States, which shall consist of a Senate and House of Representatives—Article I, Section 1, CONSTITUTION OF THE UNITED STATES

I

THE FIFTY-FIVE delegates who assembled in Philadelphia in 1789 to draw up a Constitution for the United States came from twelve states. The thirteenth—Rhode Island—had turned down an invitation to attend. Historians have noted the comparative youth of the delegates. Only four had passed the age of sixty, and Benjamin Franklin, at eighty-one, was by far the oldest. Five were under thirty and many others were in their thirties and forties. James Madison, whose ideas were to have wide influence on the convention, was only thirty-four, and Alexander Hamilton, another outstanding delegate, was thirty-two.

The fifty-five delegates were primarily men of practical experience and affairs. Most had been active in the political life of the young nation and had served in the Congress of the Confederation or in the state legislatures. Two were college presidents; another was a yeoman farmer from Georgia. Only twenty-six were college graduates, but the remaining twenty-nine were men who for one reason or another had gained notice and respect in the states they represented. Some were lawyers; others were merchants, businessmen, and men who had made money through speculation and investment. All prided themselves on their common sense and their realistic view of human nature. This realism would be reflected in every line of the Constitution they created.

The delegates had come together in Philadelphia for a specific purpose. The nation was in a crisis. Under the Articles of Confederation, which had governed the United States since the Revolution, everything was chaos and uncertainty. Public finances were in grave disorder and the credit of the country had been undermined. In order to gain tax money, the government had to have the unanimous consent of all thirteen states—an almost impossible task to accomplish. And without tax money to support its activities and policies, Congress could only remain weak and inefficient.

The weakness of America led Spain in 1784 to close the Mississippi to American ships without fear of reprisal. It likewise led in the mid-1780s to a severe economic depression, which Congress was powerless to relieve. In 1786, Daniel Shays incited a rebellion in Massachusetts among farmers alarmed by their poverty and indebtedness. The rebellion was quickly put down, but it underlined what everyone already knew. If peace and tranquillity were to be restored to the United States, the Articles of Confederation would have to be reformed. A new and stronger government with a more effective Congress would have to be established.

This was the task given to the delegates who assembled in Philadelphia. The delegates knew their work would not be easy. Under the Articles of Confederation, each of the thirteen states had enjoyed a large degree of independence. Each state jealously guarded this independence from encroachment by other states. The problem for the delegates would be to convince each state that its own best interests were served by joining a strong national union and that much of the independence each state now possessed would be preserved.

A second major problem confronted the delegates to the Constitutional Convention. They deplored the weakness of Congress under the Articles of Confederation, but at the same time they feared that any change toward a stronger government might lead to tyranny and despotism. "Wherever the real power in a government lies," wrote James Madison, "there is the danger of oppression." The solution was to steer a middle course. Grant the Congress and federal government the powers they needed to become more efficient and forceful, but stop short of giving them powers they could misuse. "In framing a government which is to be administered by men over men," Madison concluded, "the great difficulty lies in this: you must first enable the government to control the governed; and in the next place oblige it to control itself."

While the Constitutional Convention was assembled in Philadelphia, the first volume of John Adams's scholarly work, *Defense of the Constitutions of the Government of the United States*, reached the delegates. At the time, Adams was in England, where he served as envoy to the Court of St. James's, but his book nevertheless made its influence felt on several members of the convention. The book was an exhaustive investigation of the various constitutions of the American states and an inquiry into the sort of government that might best serve the United States.

Adams argued that the American government should be structured so that it represented both what he called the "aristocracy" and the "democracy." Among the aristocracy, he included the best educated, the wealthy, the great farmers, merchants, bankers, and others whose status set them apart from the rest of society.

By democracy, he meant the masses of poorer farmers, city workers, and all who made their living by labor.

Aristocracy and democracy, Adams claimed, should be made to neutralize each other's interests. This could be done by giving each faction a chamber in Congress. One chamber would be broadly representative and democratic; the other would be composed of only the wisest and ablest men, chosen from the nation's elite. Above both chambers, Adams placed a chief executive, impartial and strong, who would be able to veto the actions of Congress. An independent judiciary, owing no responsibility to the chief executive or Congress, completed the three divisions of government. This system, Adams believed, would balance the interests of rich and poor, of the elite and the masses, and prevent either group from gaining too much power at the expense of the other.

Throughout his book, Adams revealed his sympathies for the aristocracy. These sympathies were likewise held by several delegates to the convention, including Alexander Hamilton, Gouverneur Morris of Pennsylvania, and Roger Sherman of Connecticut. But there were others who leaned toward democracy. James Madison agreed with Adams that in the new government "ambition should be made to counteract ambition." Madison, however, believed that Congress and government should be able to represent and reconcile the many interest groups that would arise in a large and growing nation. It is "politic as well as just," Madison wrote, "that the interests and rights of every class should be duly represented and understood in public councils." Those who tended to agree with Madison included James Wilson of Pennsylvania and John Dickinson of Delaware.

The major difference between the two groups, the aristocrats and democrats, was one of emphasis. Although the aristocratic sympathizers were cautious and fearful of an experiment in government that gave power and responsibility to the masses, Madison and his followers hoped that it would work. Whereas the aristocrats looked upon government as a means to check and balance groups that would otherwise destroy one another out of naked self-interest, the democrats saw it as a means to extend privilege and bring the whole nation into the political arena. The views of both groups were written into the Constitution.

II

ONE OF the first orders of business the convention took up was the structure of the new Congress that would replace the Congress of the Articles of Confederation. Most delegates favored a bicameral legislature, or one with two houses. This passed the convention, seven states to three (the delegates voted by states rather than as individuals).

The next question brought the delegates into direct confrontation with the problem of aristocracy and democracy. How were the members of the two houses to be elected? James Wilson spoke in favor of a House of Representatives chosen by the people themselves. The government, he said, "ought to possess the mind and sense of the people at large." But other delegates held back from direct election, even of the House of Representatives, fearing that it would unleash the power of the mob. "The people immediately should have as little to do" with electing the government as possible, Roger Sherman claimed, because they are not well informed or educated "and are constantly liable to be misled." Sherman argued that members of the House of Representatives should be elected by the state legislatures. The more democratic delegates, however, carried the day, and the direct popular election * of members of the House won by a vote of nine states to one.

* At this time, "direct popular election" meant election by the white, male population. Black males received the vote in 1868. Women received the vote in 1920.

The next question was the Senate, which most delegates wanted to be the aristocratic branch of Congress. James Madison and James Wilson argued for direct election, but to no avail. Gouverneur Morris, one of the most conservative men at the convention, pointed out that the Senate's duty would be "to check the precipitation, changeableness, and excesses of the first branch," or House of Representatives. In order to do this, he said, the Senate would have to consist of carefully selected men who would not be subject to the whims of the people. A majority of the convention sided with Morris and decided that the Senate would be elected by members of the state legislatures.

The convention then turned its attention to the number of representatives and senators each state would be allowed to have. Delegates from the larger states, like Virginia, favored a system in which the membership of both houses would be based on the wealth of the state or upon the size of its free population. But the delegates from smaller states protested that this would be unfair and give the wealthier and more populous states an unfair advantage in Congress.

In order to placate both the large states and the small states, a compromise was reached. Membership in the House of Representatives would be based on population, with each state receiving roughly one representative for every 30,000 people.* This meant that the most populous states would have the largest delegations, whereas the thinly populated states would have small ones. At the same time, however, each state, large or small, would have two senators. Thus in one house of Congress, the larger states would

* Representation in the House was to be based on the total free population, male and female, and on three-fifths of the slave population of each state.

have the advantage, but in the other, all states would be on an equal footing. Wealth was dropped from consideration as a basis for the size of a state's delegation to Congress and a proposal to have three senators from each state was rejected because it would make the Senate too large.

How long were representatives and senators to be allowed to serve in Congress? There was strong sentiment for annual elections, because yearly elections would make it difficult for any one man to amass a great deal of power. But the delegates also recognized that yearly elections would make it difficult for representatives to gain the experience and knowledge necessary to deal with national problems. Madison proposed a three-year term, but Roger Sherman thought this too long. "The representatives ought to return home and mix with the people," he said, because "by remaining at the seat of government they would acquire the habits of the place which might differ from those of their constituents." The convention settled on a two-year term for members of the House. Terms of four, six, and eight years were considered for the Senate with the six-year term finally adopted.

The problems of qualifications for serving in the House of Representatives and the Senate were likewise debated by the convention. Twenty-five was chosen as the minimum age for representatives, and thirty as the minimum age for senators. These relatively young ages reflected the comparative youth of many of the delegates. To be elected, members of Congress likewise had to be inhabitants of the states from which they were elected and had to be citizens of the United States. Representatives were required to have been citizens for at least seven years; nine years of citizenship was required of senators.

The convention voted down all property qualifications for holding office in Congress. This was surprising, because most of the delegates were men of wealth and substance and because most state laws of the time required members of their state legislatures to own property or possess a certain amount of wealth. John Dickinson spoke for the majority when he said that "the policy of interweaving into a Republican Constitution a veneration of wealth" was dangerous and could lead to a situation in which men of talent and ability were excluded from holding office simply because they were poor. Nor was religion of any kind held necessary for membership in Congress, although most states at this time required religious affiliations on the part of state officials. Indeed, the delegates accepted without dissent a statement that read, "No religious test shall ever be required as a qualification to any office or public trust under the United States."

The convention directed that representatives and senators be paid from the national treasury; this was done to assure that members of Congress would owe loyalty only to the federal government and the people of the United States. It likewise gave Congress the right to "be judge of the elections, returns, and qualifications of its own members" so that disputed elections would be resolved by Congress itself rather than by any outside body.

The independence of Congress was further assured by a provision in the Constitution that required each house to determine "the rules of its proceedings, punish its members for disorderly behavior, and, with the concurrence of two-thirds, expel a member." This provision meant that Congress would be allowed to determine the course of its own development. Because no exact rules of procedure were laid down, both the House and Senate could change their rules to suit changing times and respond to new problems as they arose. Finally, the Constitution obligated each house to "keep a journal, and from time to time publish the same." This was done, in the words of James Wilson, so that the people would be able to know "what their agents are doing or have done."

III

ONCE THE structure of the Congress had been settled, the next great question before the convention was the kinds of power it would grant the House of Representatives and the Senate. This was the most difficult problem the delegates had to debate and the one that aroused the greatest controversy throughout the nation. How much power should be taken from the states in order to strengthen the federal government? How much power could Congress or the federal government handle safely, without becoming tyrannical and despotic?

As we saw in the first chapter, the most important power the Constitution granted Congress was the authority to tax and to spend, the so-called power of the purse. This power it turned over to the House of Representatives because that was the house elected directly by the people and therefore more deeply aware of their concerns and needs. "No money shall be drawn from the Treasury, but in consequence of appropriations made by law," the Constitution read, and "all bills for raising revenue shall originate in the House of Representatives; but the Senate may propose or concur with amendments as on other bills." The money spent by Congress should be used "to pay the debts and provide for the common defense and general welfare of the United States. . . ."

The power to tax included all known forms of taxation such as tariffs on goods imported from abroad and excises on the manufacture, sale, use, or transfer of property within the United States. The Constitution required, however, that taxes be uniform throughout the country and that no section be taxed unfairly. After 1913, when the Sixteenth Amendment was ratified, Congress also had the right to tax the personal incomes of American citizens.* The income tax provided a large new source of money for the federal budget.

The power to tax is an impressive power, but Congress devotes far more of its time to the question of spending the money it has raised. One expert has estimated that nine-tenths of the working time of Congress is spent, directly or indirectly, with appropriations. Appropriations can include bills of personal interest to a representative or senator, such as money for a dam or public works project for his district or state. They can likewise include money to be spent for national problems, like military buildup, health insurance, or foreign aid. Because the Constitution allows Congress to borrow money for the United States, this problem too comes up for frequent congressional consideration. Critics point out that the Constitution places no limits on the amount of money Congress can borrow and that this has led to an enormous national debt of three-quarters of a trillion dollars. Others, however, argue that the power to borrow is a necessary function of government and that without it Congress would be hard pressed to find the money it needs.

When it came to the powers Congress would have over commerce, the Constitutional Convention was vague. The formula gave no precise statement of authority or definition of terms. "The Congress shall have power . . . to regulate commerce with foreign nations," the Constitution read, "and among the several states, and with the Indian tribes." But where did the federal power begin and that of the states come to an end? How much authority would Congress be allowed to wield before it violated its prerogatives and became dictatorial?

* An income tax was first levied in 1862 to help the government meet expenses during the Civil War. The Supreme Court at first accepted the tax, but in 1895 declared it unconstitutional. This decision led to the constitutional amendment that allowed Congress to tax personal income.

These questions were left for the Supreme Court and experience to decide. In 1824, under Chief Justice John Marshall, the Court handed down its first great decision concerning the powers of Congress to regulate commerce. Marshall interpreted the authority of Congress broadly. The power of Congress is supreme, he wrote, when it deals with commerce carried on among states. Only when some aspect of commercial life is carried on completely within the boundaries of a state does that state have the right to pass regulatory laws.

With the power of Congress declared supreme in interstate commerce, the next question to be settled was the definition of the word *commerce*. At first, the Supreme Court ruled that manufacturing and production concerns were not included under commerce. But after 1887, when Congress passed the first Interstate Commerce Act, and especially in the twentieth century, the Court has viewed any activities that have "an effect on commerce" as under the jurisdiction of Congress. Gradually, the authority of the federal government was extended until 1946, when the Court declared that "the federal commerce power is as broad as the economic needs of the nation." With that decision, the stage was set for the extraordinary authority Congress now exercises in the area of the nation's commercial life.

Under its powers to regulate commerce, Congress has moved to control the rates the public is charged by transportation companies, electric and other utility firms, and to control the development of nuclear energy. It has also used its commercial regulatory authority to put an end to child labor and to help secure equal rights for black citizens. To oversee commerce, Congress has established the "big seven" regulatory agencies: Interstate Commerce Commission, Federal Trade Commission, Federal Power Commission, Federal Communication Commission, Securities and Exchange Commission, National Labor Relations Board, and Civil Aeronautics Board. From their names, it is evident that Congress has spread its authority over many aspects of the nation's commercial life. These commissions and boards, in the words of the late Speaker of the House, Sam Rayburn, are the "creatures of Congress," established for the sole purpose of seeing that all the regulatory laws passed by the House and Senate are carried out.

As we saw in the first chapter, the most awesome duty that Congress must perform is to declare war. Some members of the Constitutional Convention, like Pierce Butler of South Carolina, wanted to place the war-making power entirely in the hands of the chief executive "who will have all the requisite qualities and will not make war but when the nation will support it." Others, however, viewed this position with suspicion. If the President had the sole power to make war, who would be able to control his power if he should involve the country in an unnecessary or unpopular war? Therefore the convention granted Congress as a whole the right "to declare war," but it was left to the President to act in time of emergency in order to repel a sudden attack. In the words of Roger Sherman, "The executive should be able to repel, and not commence war."

The convention also granted Congress the power to "raise and support armies" and "to provide and maintain a navy." But because the delegates had a deep distrust of a standing army—an army maintained in time of peace as well as war—two important safeguards against the misuse of military power were written into the Constitution. The first made it impossible for Congress to appropriate funds for the military for a period of more than two years. This gave the House and Senate the chance to review and alter, if necessary, military spending and practice.

The second provision designed to control the power of a standing army allowed Congress "to provide for organizing, arming, and disciplining the militia and for governing such part of them as may be employed in the service of the United States. In the eyes of the delegates to the Constitutional Convention, the militia was an attractive alternative to a large army. Because it was composed of men who pursued other professions but who were trained in warfare and could come together at a moment's notice, it did not create the same threat to liberty and free institutions that a standing army did. An army might get out of control and use its power to govern; a militia might better be kept under the guidance of Congress.

Other powers the convention granted Congress included the power to conduct investigations and the right to initiate amendments to the Constitution.* Also included were lesser but nevertheless important powers like the authority to admit new states into the Union, to coin money, issue copyrights, establish post offices, issue provisions concerning bankruptcy procedures and the naturalization of new citizens, and provide for a seat of government, eventually in Washington, D. C.

Finally, the Constitution gives Congress the power "to make all laws which shall be necessary and proper for carrying into execution the foregoing powers, and all other powers vested by this Constitution in the government of the United States, or in any department or officer thereof." This has been called the "sweeping clause" because, at first glance, it seemed vague and ambiguous. Did it mean that Congress could expand its powers when it deemed new powers "necessary and proper"? Or did it mean simply that Congress had the right to make new laws only when those laws were connected with powers it had already been *specifically* granted? Most constitutional scholars and historians believe that the latter was the case. The "sweeping clause" granted no new powers to Congress, they argue, but only reinforced the powers it already had.

* The states likewise have the power to initiate amendments, but this has never been done. The present twenty-six amendments to the Constitution originated in Congress after which they were approved by three-quarters of the states before ratification.

IV

ONE OF the most complex problems the delegates to the Constitutional Convention had to deal with was the relationship that would exist between the chief executive and the Congress. Was one branch of government to be superior to the other? Or were they to be equal in power and, if so, how was this equality to be established?

Roger Sherman believed that the President should be nothing "more than an institution for carrying the will of the legislature into effect." He favored a weak chief executive who would simply supervise and implement the laws passed by Congress. Gouverneur Morris, on the other hand, spoke for those who wanted a strong and vigorous chief executive when he said the President should be "the guardian of the people" against any possible tyranny that might be exercised by Congress. Morris and his supporters wanted an executive endowed with powers strong enough to check and neutralize the powers of Congress.

In the plan that was adopted, the convention established an office of chief executive to be held by one man to be called the President. The President would be chosen by electors from each state; the number of electors would equal the total number of representatives and senators from each state. The convention rejected a move to give the chief executive the title "His Highness," because that title smacked of royalty and was not in keeping with democracy. It likewise rejected a plan to give the nation three presidents because three presidents would inevitably quarrel with one another. Also discussed was a plan to have the President elected by Congress, but this was discarded because of the danger of "intrigue and faction" that might arise when it came time to select a new chief executive.

The convention granted the chief executive broad authority,

but checked and balanced his power with that of Congress. The President could veto bills passed by the House of Representatives and Senate, but his veto could be overridden by a two-thirds vote of both houses. He was likewise given the right to appoint ambassadors and other officials and to make treaties with foreign nations, but only with the advice and consent of the Senate. In no sphere of activity was the President's power made absolute. Even his title, Commander in Chief of the armed forces, was balanced by the congressional duty to "provide for the common defense," "to raise and support armies," and to "maintain a navy."

These shared powers have sometimes led to antagonism between the chief executive and the Congress and to a constitutional problem that has never been resolved: how to maintain a steady balance of power between the legislative branch of government and the executive. Strong Presidents have swung the balance of power in their direction; strong Congresses have swung it in the other. Periods of cooperation have been relatively rare. In recent years, after a long period of strong presidential authority, Congress has once again chosen to assert its power in many directions, including the making of foreign policy, an area of government activity usually regarded as the prerogative of the President.

As the third branch of government, the Constitutional Convention established an independent judiciary consisting of a Supreme Court and lower courts. The court system could decide the constitutionality of presidential activities and of bills passed by Congress, with the Supreme Court as the source of final appeal on all constitutional and legal questions. The President was given the power to appoint judges to the courts, but his appointments had to be confirmed by the Senate. Thus in this instance too the President had to share his powers with Congress. Presidents have usually sought to get the men they wanted on the Supreme Court, but in the matter of appointments to the lesser federal courts, they have often nominated persons suggested to them by members of

Congress in order to gain favor from individual representatives and senators.

The Constitution granted Congress one power that made it potentially more powerful than the President or the courts. This was the power of impeachment. This meant that any government official, charged with and convicted of misbehavior or misconduct in office, could be removed from office by an action of Congress. The power to impeach was given to the House of Representatives; the power to try these officials and remove them from office was given to the Senate.

In order to prevent members of Congress from removing a public official simply because they found him or his policies personally disagreeable, the Constitution listed treason, bribery, and other "high crimes and misdemeanors" as misdeeds worthy of impeachment. Otherwise, as Charles Pinckney of South Carolina pointed out, should the President oppose "a favorite law" or bill of Congress, "the two houses will combine against him, and under the influence of heat or faction, throw him out of office."

Because the power of impeachment is serious and difficult to complete, it has seldom been used. Two Presidents have faced impeachment, Andrew Johnson and Richard Nixon. Johnson was impeached by the House and came within one vote of being convicted by the Senate. Nixon resigned from office before the impeachment proceedings could begin. The House, however, has impeached thirteen federal officers, six of whom resigned or were removed from office. All of those removed from office were judges who had been charged with a variety of offenses, including intoxication in office, support for the South during the Civil War, and bribery.

In several instances, the Constitutional Convention was concerned with limiting the power of Congress to assure that it would never have the power to destroy individual liberty. Several of these concerns derived from the American experience before the

Revolution, when English rule had seemed distant and arbitrary. Therefore the Constitution guaranteed that "the privilege of a writ of habeas corpus cannot be suspended, unless when in cases of rebellion or invasion the public safety may require it." The Constitution likewise barred all bills of attainder and ex post facto laws.* Taken together, these three provisions were designed to confine the rights of Congress and of the government and to guard against what John Adams called the natural tendency of government to grow and expand its powers unless checked.

This desire to control and check the powers of Congress also led to the adoption of the first ten amendments to the Constitution, which are known as the Bill of Rights. These amendments were added in the months after the close of the convention so that the states would have no fears about a despotic federal government and would ratify and accept the Constitution. The first declared that "Congress shall make no law respecting an establishment of religion, or prohibiting the free exercise thereof; or abridging the freedom of speech, or of the press; or of the right of the people peaceably to assemble, and to petition the government for a redress of grievances." The others guaranteed the right of citizens to bear arms, protected them from "unreasonable searches and seizures," allowed for a "speedy public trial" in criminal prosecutions, and so on.

The Constitution drawn up in Philadelphia in 1787 represented a series of compromises among the delegates at the convention.

* Writs of habeas corpus have as their object to bring a party before a court or judge for trial. A bill of attainder is a legislative act that inflicts the consequences of attainder—or loss of civil rights—without judicial trial. Ex post facto laws are laws passed after an event, but retroactive upon it. Thus an ex post facto law can result in the arrest of someone who committed an act legal at the time it was committed, but declared illegal at a later time.

Those who wanted a strong federal government to replace the weak government under the Articles of Confederation were pleased by the numerous powers granted Congress, the authority of the President, and the independent judiciary. Those who feared centralized government, on the other hand, were satisfied by the limits of power defined by the Constitution, by the elaborate system of checks and balances it established, and by the addition of the Bill of Rights.

The system of checks and balances was at the core of the new government. Each of the three branches of government—the legislative, the executive, and the judiciary—had powers of its own, but the potential for misuse of these powers was lessened by the power each branch of government had over the others. The President could veto a bill passed by Congress, but Congress could override that veto by a two-thirds vote of both houses. The President could appoint judges and government officials, but these appointments were subject to the approval of the Senate. The President could conduct foreign affairs and was commander in chief of the armed forces, but Congress also had a say in these matters.

The elaborate system of checks and balances was reflected in the way the Constitution structured Congress. On the one hand, the House of Representatives was designed to represent the democratic forces of the new nation. Its members were elected by direct vote, unlike any other officials of the government, and were subject to the wishes of the masses. The purpose of the Senate, on the other hand, was aristocratic and elitist. The Senate, Gouverneur Morris declared, "will show us the might of aristocracy" against the less cultivated and less educated members of the House. For James Madison, however, the duty of the upper house was first "to protect the people against their rulers; secondly to protect the people against the transient impressions into which they themselves might be led." For, Madison continued, the people, as well as the "numerous" House of Representatives, could err and make mistakes out of "fickleness and passion." But the Senate, composed of a "select portion of enlightened citizens," would serve as "a necessary fence against this danger" and "with firmness might seasonably interpose against impetuous councils." Thus the House might voice the desires of the people, but the Senate would temper these desires with wisdom and consideration.

The Founding Fathers hoped to establish a government that would secure the blessings of liberty and freedom for the American people, but they were not idealists. They believed human beings tended to be greedy and to be governed by self-interest, and they sought to create a government in which these tendencies could be checked and brought under control. The Constitution was based on realism and experience rather than on utopian dreams. Indeed, many of the Founding Fathers doubted that the system they had established would work. John Adams wrote, "Democracy never lasts long. It soon wastes, exhausts, and murders itself." And Benjamin Franklin, when asked by a woman what kind of government the Constitutional Convention had created, responded, "A republic, madam, if you can keep it."

CHAPTER THREE

THE HOUSE IN PRACTICE

The House of Representatives is one of the most complicated legislatures in the world. Observers, sympathetic and otherwise, have remarked on the buzzing confusion that seems to characterize its workings—Roger Davidson and Walter Oleszek, CONGRESS AGAINST ITSELF

THE CONSTITUTION enumerated the powers and authority granted to the House of Representatives. It laid down qualifications for membership and spelled out the method of election for those who might seek office in the House. But beyond these basic laws, the Constitution said little except that "the House of Representatives shall choose their Speaker and other officers." The Founding Fathers assumed that the House would work with the traditions long established by the English Parliament. These traditions were familiar to the early Americans because they had been adopted by the legislatures of the original colonies and were later the basis for the procedures used by the Constitutional Convention.

Besides the English parliamentary tradition, two other general factors have influenced the development of the House. These were its rapid growth in size in the nineteenth century and the increased workload borne by every representative in the twentieth century. From its original fifty-nine members, the House has grown to 435 men and women of diverse origins, backgrounds, and interests. The problem faced by the House has been to mold these 435 men and women into an effective law-making body and to keep time-consuming disputes and controversies at a minimum. The tendency of the House to become decentralized and disorganized has had to be balanced by an effort to emphasize the general will of the membership and to create a coherent policy-making body out of its diverse makeup.

Increased workloads too have played their part in the evolution of House practice. The first House of Representatives had only 142 bills to consider, whereas current Houses have many thousands. In 1973 and 1974, for instance, the House introduced 6,901 bills. These bills are not only numerous, but they also deal with many complex issues, from abortion to nuclear energy, on which opinion is largely divided. This has meant that the modern member of Congress must be knowledgeable on a wide range of issues and must rely on staff and aides to keep him or her abreast of the problems at hand. The staff of the first House was almost nonexistent; today's House, by comparison, has a staff of more than 13,500.

The three principal divisions of House practice are leadership, rules, and committees. Over the years, the House has divided its attention among developments in these three fields, sometimes emphasizing changes in one area, sometimes in another. We shall look into each area separately, but with the understanding that the three areas overlap and cannot be completely divorced from one another.

I

WHEN THE first House of Representatives assembled in 1789, its first order of business was the election of a Speaker of the House.

Most of the representatives were familiar with the office because they had served in state legislatures where parliamentary procedure was observed. The Speaker's primary duty was to preside over the House while it conducted its business. He was to preserve decorum and order—a sometimes difficult task, especially in the early years of the House—and decide on all points of order that arose. He was to put questions before the House for consideration and to announce the results of votes on bills. Clearly these were powers that could give a strong man a great deal of authority.

Several men who served as Speaker of the House have deeply influenced the development of that office. The first was Henry Clay, who is the only representative to have been chosen Speaker the day he entered Congress. Clay believed that a Speaker should display "patience, good temper, and courtesy" toward the House membership and that he should "remain cool and unshaken amidst all the storms of debate, carefully guarding the preservation of the permanent laws and rules of the House from being sacrificed to temporary passions, prejudices, or interests."

Clay is best remembered, however, for the way he wielded power. He established the office of Speaker as a political post, using his great skills to advance his own political philosophy. He entered House debates, where his eloquence won him many supporters, and exercised his right to vote on bills along with his colleagues. He believed that it was his responsibility to make "the best arrangement and distribution of the talent of the House," by which he meant he used his power to see that people who agreed with his views were appointed to important committees. Thus Clay saw his role as Speaker as twofold. He was the presiding officer of the House of Representatives, but he was at the same time the leader of the political party that had placed him in power.

This concept of the speakership was to have strong influence on the history of the House. Clay's last term as Speaker ended in 1825, and the prestige of the House along with that of its leader went into decline shortly afterward. But in the years after the Civil War, Clay's precedent was once again revived and has played an important part in the life of Congress since that time. The next strong Speaker, James G. Blaine (Republican, Maine), who served between 1869 and 1875, made it clear where his loyalties were. "Chosen by the party representing the political majority," he told the House, "the Speaker owes a faithful allegiance to the principles and policy of that party."

In the years after Blaine, the powers of the Speaker grew rapidly. Blaine initiated the process by making new use of the Speaker's right to appoint committees. For most earlier Speakers, this had been a routine process, often based on seniority. Blaine, however, calculated the needs of his own legislative program and made his appointments to further the good of that program. People who might delay his policies were passed over, while his friends received important posts. Blaine tightened his control over representatives who were members of his own party so as to strengthen party discipline and increase his control over recalcitrant representatives.

In the 1880s and 1890s, two other Speakers, both of them skilled parliamentarians, used their power and knowledge of House procedures to keep order in the often unruly Houses of their time. John Carlisle (Democrat, Kentucky) exercised the Speaker's "right of recognition." House rules said that when two or more representatives rose at one time to be recognized "the Speaker shall name who is first to speak." Carlisle decided that he could save time by simply asking, "For what purpose does the gentleman rise?" If the representative indicated that he wanted to delay the business at hand, Carlisle would turn to someone else.

Carlisle's tactic helped to increase the efficiency of the House and to speed up the consideration of bills. But it was the tactics of his immediate successor, Thomas Reed, that gave the House a sense of order and direction that had been unusual in its history.

A large, impressive man, Reed was known for his sharp wit and his frequent criticism of House procedures. "The object of a parliamentary body is action, and not stoppage of action," he once observed. "Hence, if any Member or set of Members undertakes to oppose the orderly process of business, even by the use of the ordinarily recognized parliamentary motions, it is the right of the majority to refuse to have those motions entertained, and to cause the public business to proceed. . . ."

Reed's tactics altered House practice as it had never been altered in the past. He completely revised the order of business, outlawed delaying motions, and made several other changes designed to speed up business and weaken the power of the opposition. Because he was chairman of the important Rules Committee, Reed could control the timing and content of all the bills before the House. No legislation or House procedure was beyond his power, and he rarely hesitated to exercise his power.

One of Reed's most striking moves was against what was known as the disappearing quorum.* For years, representatives who opposed a certain piece of legislation would refuse to vote on that legislation when it came up for consideration, even though they were present in the House when the vote was taken. By declining to vote, the representatives were deemed "not present"—thereby dissolving the quorum that had previously existed and bringing business to a halt.

On a key vote on January 29, 1890, Reed overcame the practice of a disappearing quorum by exercising his own authority as Speaker to decide what would officially constitute a quorum. The question at hand involved a disputed election race in West Virginia. On this issue 161 Republicans—members of Reed's own party—had voted yes, two representatives had voted no, and 165,

* A quorum, usually an absolute majority, is the number of members of Congress needed to be present in order for the House or Senate to be legally competent to conduct business and to pass legislation.

mostly Democrats, had not voted either way, although they were present.

At this point, Reed directed the clerk of the House "to record the following names of members present and refusing to vote." He then listed the names of thirty-eight representatives he recognized on the House floor. With the addition of these names, Reed declared that a quorum was present and that business could proceed. The House immediately dissolved in uproar, and the legality of Reed's tactics was hotly debated for three days. In the end, he was upheld, but only after a vote along strict party lines.

Reed was denounced as a "tyrant" and "czar" by his enemies, who believed that he had given the Speaker and the majority party in the House too much power at the expense of the minority. But he defended his tactics against the disappearing quorum and his other actions in a letter to his constituents in Maine. "If we have broken the precedents of a hundred years," he wrote, "we have set the precedents of another hundred years nobler than the last, wherein the people, with full knowledge that their servants can act, will choose those who will worthily carry out their will."

Reed ruled the House with the help of trusted lieutenants who helped him carry out his will. One of these lieutenants was Joseph Cannon of Illinois, who became Speaker on his own in 1903 and held the office until 1910. Cannon took advantage of the tradition of a strong speakership established by Blaine, Carlisle, and Reed and exercised more authority in his office than any other Speaker has ever done. By 1909, he was regarded as a dictator, especially by the minority Democrats, but also by many members of his own Republican party.

Cannon used the powers bequeathed to him by his predecessors, but used them more extensively. He dominated the Rules Committee and made it do his bidding. He made appointments to important committees as he saw fit, and he controlled the procedures of the House for the benefit of his party. But as the years passed, his leadership grew more erratic. He was a conservative Republican at a time when a period of change had come to the nation, and he tended to rule his party by the tenets of an earlier philosophy, rather than to allow for the new and different.

During his last years as Speaker, opposition to Cannon's leadership became more open and visible. No one voiced this dissatisfaction better than John Nelson (Republican, Wisconsin). "Have we not been punished by every means at the disposal of the powerful House organization?" Nelson complained. "Members long chairmen of important committees, others holding high rank—all with records of faithful and efficient party service to their credit—have been ruthlessly removed, deposed and humiliated before their constituents and the country, because forsooth, they would not cringe or crawl before the arbitrary power of the Speaker and his House machine." What most representatives wanted, Nelson concluded, was the "common right of equal representation in this House, and the right of way of progressive legislation in Congress."

The revolt against "Cannonism" began in 1909. House rebels were unable to get enough votes to remove Cannon from the office of Speaker, but they did make several minor changes in House rules that eventually spelled his doom. The first was a provision for a "unanimous consent calendar." This device allowed House members to schedule noncontroversial bills as a part of House routine, freeing them from the need to appeal to the Speaker for the right to bring up any bill, controversial or noncontroversial.

The second device instituted by the rebels was "Calendar Wednesday." Under Calendar Wednesday, the names of all House committees were to be called alphabetically each Wednesday, at which time the committee chairmen would be allowed to introduce nonprivileged legislation reported by their committees. This meant that many minor bills could bypass the Rules Committee—of which Cannon was chairman—and reach the House floor free of his jurisdiction. It was a small step against the authority of the Speaker, but nevertheless an important one.

Cannon attempted to sidestep Calendar Wednesday by arranging to have it set aside each week so that more important legislation could be considered. House rebels, however, had reached the point where they would not permit their movement to be so easily thwarted. On Wednesday, March 16, 1910, the fight was on. As usual, Cannon attempted to avoid Calendar Wednesday by moving on to more privileged business—a discussion of the census that was to be taken that year. A point of order was called, which Cannon overruled. The rebels then appealed this ruling on the grounds that Calendar Wednesday could be set aside only by a two-thirds vote of the House.

In the debate that followed, the rebels claimed that the Speaker was disrupting the flow of House business, because he had refused to allow the consideration of nonprivileged bills to take place. Cannon stood his ground and said that he was working entirely within the precedents established by earlier Speakers. If the House should decide to overrule his decision, he added, it would "make it plain that he has no more and no less authority than any Speaker who has preceded him." By a vote of 163 to 112 (with 113 abstaining or voting "present"), however, Cannon was defeated.

The next day, George Norris (Republican, Nebraska), one of the rebels, moved for a change in the Rules Committee, one of Cannon's most important sources of power. Norris wanted the Rules Committee changed from the present five-man committee of which the Speaker was chairman to a fifteen-member committee, independent of the Speaker. The new committee, Norris said, should be elected by the full House and apportioned geographically, with members representing all parts of the country. The members would choose their own chairman and, in turn, have the right to appoint the members of every standing committee.

A Cannon supporter, John Dalzell (Republican, Pennsylvania), raised a point of order against Norris's motion, and the debate was on. For four days, arguments were heard on both sides of the issue. Cannon justified his authority by pointing out that a powerful Speaker helped the House to get things done. "Results cannot be had except by a majority," he said, "and in the House of Representatives a majority, being responsible, should have full power and should exercise that power; otherwise the majority is inefficient and does not perform its function." Cannon's critics, on the other hand, argued that the House needed less efficiency—if efficiency meant Cannon's dictatorship—and more democracy, where larger numbers of representatives could make their opinions heard.

When the point of order against Norris's motion came up for a decision, Cannon ruled in favor of the point of order. The House, however, overruled this decision by a vote of 182 to 162 (with 37 not voting and seven voting "present"). It was a marked defeat for the powerful Speaker, who was now likewise stripped of the chairmanship of the Rules Committee. Norris reintroduced a simpler bill that called for a ten-member Rules Committee, with six members from the majority party and four from the minority. The new bill deprived the Speaker of his right to chair the committee and to appoint its members. When it passed the House by a vote of 191 to 156, Cannon's authority was demolished and the days of the all-powerful Speaker were over.

The defeat of Cannon was an important event in the history of the House of Representatives. It brought an end to the method of House organization and practice, under strong central leadership, that had developed since the days of the Civil War and led to an expansion of the role and power of committee chairmen. Instead of centralized authority, the House opted for a system where authority was shared by a few senior representatives, each of whom jealously guarded his own sphere of power and activity. As Cannon had predicted, this meant that the majority party could no longer put forth a consistent and unified program for the House to consider.

During the first ten years after Cannon's fall, this trend was not so obvious. Power at first shifted to party caucuses,* where representatives of each party met with other representatives of the same party to decide on programs of legislation. Party loyalty was considered binding on all party members, especially by the Democrats, who controlled the House after 1911. When the Democrats also won the White House in the election of 1912, House Democratic leaders worked closely with the new President, Woodrow Wilson, to develop policy and the new President, in turn, relied on the caucus to support his programs. For a while, rule by caucus had replaced the authority of the Speaker.

During Wilson's second administration (1917–1921), however, the influence of the caucus began to disappear. There were two reasons for this. First, the caucus was too large to be a viable source of party unity and coherence in the House. From 250 to 300 or more members—the size of the majority party's caucus—were simply too many to mold into a single voice. And second, many representatives resented the loss of independence caucus ruled entailed. If party loyalty prevailed, they lost the right to vote against issues their own consciences opposed or that were against the interests of their constituents.

As the power of the caucus declined, the power of the important committee chairmen rose. The chairman of the Rules Committee, for instance, came to exercise more authority than in the days of Reed and Cannon, when the Speaker chaired the committee. The chairman of Rules could oppose the policies of his own

* The word *caucus*, meaning a meeting of party leaders or members to decide policy, is probably of Algonquian origin. Caucuses have been used since the beginning of Congress, but only rarely have they dominated the political system as they did during this period.

party, and frequently did. He could likewise choose to ignore a bill passed by his own committee, simply by refusing to introduce it in the House. But Rules was only one influential committee among several that included Ways and Means, Appropriations, and later, Armed Services, Interior, and others.

Joseph Cannon had little sympathy with the reforms that had altered Congress. "How times have changed!" he said in later years. "Nowadays a Speaker is expected to be nothing more than a Sunday school teacher, to pat all the good little boys on the head and turn the other cheek when the bad boys use him as a target for their bean shooter." Strong men have held the office of Speaker since Cannon's time, like Nicholas Longworth (Republican, Ohio) and Sam Rayburn,* but their power and influence have never equaled Cannon's.

II

WHEN THE first House of Representatives met on April 1, 1789, its initial order of business was the election of a Speaker. The next day, the new Speaker, Frederick Muhlenberg of Pennsylvania, named an eleven-member committee to draw up a set of rules to govern House proceedings. Rules had been a part of parliamentary practice for centuries. They were essential because they imposed order and regularity on the law-making process and because they promoted efficiency and saved time. Without an accepted set of rules, the House of Representatives or any similar organization would dissolve in no time into a body of bickering delegates unable to reach a consensus on any issue.

* The House has recognized the significance of its important Speakers by naming its office buildings after Cannon, Longworth, and Rayburn. It is a shame that no building has been named for Reed, perhaps the ablest of them all.

The rules of the House of Representatives, however, have developed into an unusually complex system of precedents and customs. In this book, we can only touch on this complexity. In 1935 the precedents alone filled nine large volumes, and there have been many new precedents added since that time. Most House members do not have a working knowledge of the complete set of rules and must appeal to the House parliamentarian's office for information. On the other hand, the few representatives who have mastered the rules have been able to use that mastery to gain power and influence over the flow of legislation.

The number and complexity of its rules have made the House a highly regulated and structured organization. Elaborate and often tedious procedures must be followed to introduce a bill and guide it through the various stages it must complete before it becomes a law. These procedures are meant to ensure that each bill will receive the best consideration and attention the House can offer, but they also have another result. Opponents of bills can use House regulations and rules to delay passage of the bill, severely water down its contents, or destroy its chances of becoming law, even when the bill is supported by a majority of representatives.

Fortunately, however, the body of rules and customs that governs the House is not rigid and inflexible. From time to time, rules have been changed and customs altered to fit new needs and circumstances. This is especially true when the rules seem to bog down legislation that is strongly favored by a sizable number of House members. In these periods—and there have been several in the history of the House, as we shall soon see—hopes run high that a change in procedures will break the invisible barrier that prevents the passage of popular legislation and allow that legislation to become law. On occasion, these hopes have been fulfilled and the legislation has passed. On others, however, they have proved illusory. As one Washington observer has put it, new rules and regulations do not necessarily mean that the House will make wiser and better decisions.

The first rules developed by the House of Representatives were relatively simple and direct. Members could not introduce bills—this was the prerogative of the Speaker—and could not speak more than twice to the same question without permission from the House. All representatives were required to vote if present in the House, unless excused, and barred from voting only if not present or if they had a direct personal involvement in the issue at hand.

The forum for considering and perfecting legislation was to be the "Committee of the Whole House." The Committee of the Whole House was simply the House under another name and was a parliamentary device used to facilitate the handling of legislation. While the Committee of the Whole House was in session, someone other than the Speaker presided, and the final consideration of a bill could be rendered without undue interruption and frustration.

All major legislative proposals began in the Committee of the Whole House. The Committee at first discussed the proposals and reached a general agreement on the questions involved. Then the proposal was turned over to a select committee * whose duty it was to draft the particulars of the bill. After the select committee had carefully drawn up the bill, it was returned to the House, where the Committee of the Whole House debated the legislation part by part. The Committee of the Whole House could then vote to accept the bill, to reject it, or to modify it by adding amendments. This done, the Committee of the Whole House was dissolved, and the Speaker resumed the chair. The House now

* A *select committee* is one appointed to complete a given task after which it is dissolved. A *standing committee* is one whose appointment is permanent and which continues to exist, Congress after Congress.

voted to accept or reject the bill. This action was followed by a third and final reading of the completed or "engrossed" bill and final passage or rejection by the House.

These procedures, however, soon proved awkward and cumbersome. There were two reasons for this. First, the House of Representatives grew rapidly in the years after the first Congress * and there soon were too many members for business to be conducted in this manner. And second, even though the rules limited the number of times a representative could speak on a certain bill, they did not limit the *length of time* he could speak. This led to the practice of filibustering. When a representative or a group of representatives opposed a bill, they could "talk it to death" by taking the floor and refusing to give it up.

As political parties made their appearance and partisanship began to grow, the filibusters grew longer and longer. The champion filibusterer of the early House was Barent Gardener (Federalist, New York) who once spoke continuously against a bill for twenty-four hours. Other House members proved equally clever at finding ways to tie up business and make their opinions felt.

The House devised several new parliamentary tactics to meet these problems. In 1811, for instance, it was decided that a majority could shut off debate on a bill by calling for the "previous question," a move that made any effort to filibuster out of order. This rule became standard practice in the House in spite of the opposition of prominent members like John Randolph, who regarded it as a "gag rule," and others like Thomas Hart Benton, who claimed that it did "permanent injury" to the right of freedom of debate.

In the same year, a rule to establish a new and more efficient daily order of business was adopted, and in 1817 another rule

* The House had fifty-nine members in 1789. After the first census, in 1790, this was nearly doubled to 106. The House grew to 142 in 1800, to 186 in 1810, and to 213 in 1820.

made it possible for the House to protect itself from business it did not wish to take up, a move that helped the membership to concentrate on matters it considered essential to the national welfare and ignore lesser matters that took up valuable time. Moreover, by 1820, steps had been taken to limit the time a representative could speak on a given bill to one hour.* In 1847, this was reduced to five minutes, an indication of how difficult it had become to carry on business. And finally, in 1860, the House further limited the time allowed for discussion by ruling that a majority could prohibit all debate on any amendments offered to a bill.

These efforts, however, did not destroy the power of representatives who might want to disrupt House business. The flow of legislation could still be brought to an abrupt halt by a group of determined representatives using the full arsenal of parliamentary maneuvers available to them. This was the case, for instance, during the heated debate that raged around the Kansas-Nebraska bill of 1854.† Asher Hinds (Republican, Maine), a supporter of the bill, has left us this description of the tactics used by the opponents. They engaged, he wrote, in "prolonged dilatory operations, such as the alternation of the motions to lay on the table, for a call of the House, to excuse individual members from voting, to adjourn, to reconsider votes whereby individual members were excused from voting, to adjourn, to fix the day to which the House should adjourn, and, after calls of the House had been ordered, to excuse individual absentees." These "dilatory operations" took up 109 House roll calls and wasted many days of activity. It was pre-

* This rule was proposed when John Randolph spoke for more than four hours on one bill. It did not become fully accepted until 1841.

† The Kansas-Nebraska bill called for the recognition of those two areas as territories within the United States. The question that divided the House, as well as the Senate and the nation, was whether or not slavery would be declared legal in the new territories.

cisely the sort of thing the House had striven to overcome and would continue to try to surmount in the future.

The Kansas-Nebraska bill involved the highly controversial issue of slavery, which had divided Congress and the nation for many years and would lead to civil war. As early as 1792, the House had moved to skirt the problem by ruling that it would not receive petitions that questioned the existence of slavery. This rule was honored until 1836, when John Quincy Adams, the only former President to serve in the House after his presidency, presented a document from his home state of Massachusetts that called for the abolition of slavery in the District of Columbia.

At first, the House of Representatives simply refused to consider or act upon the petition. But the next year, representatives from the southern states, where slavery was practiced, began a move to censure Adams. The attempt at censure failed, but the House did agree that "slaves do not have the right of petition" that is granted to other Americans under the Constitution. The question, however, continued to plague the House, which voted in 1840 never to consider the abolition of slavery and then, in 1844, reversed itself and declared that slavery could indeed be challenged in the House. But in large part, it was Adams's original move in 1836 that undermined more than forty years of accepted practice and procedure. His act was an example of how seemingly rigid rules can be changed by the courage of one representative.

On several occasions in its history, the House of Representatives has undertaken a general reassessment of its rules and customs. One such reassessment was initiated in 1858 and completed two years later.* Another, more complete reassessment was made in 1880 under the guidance of Speaker Samuel Randall (Demo-

* House procedure had been improved in 1837 with the adoption of Thomas Jefferson's *Manual of Parliamentary Procedure*. Jefferson's *Manual* had been adopted much earlier by the Senate.

crat, Pennsylvania), who declared that the guiding principle behind reform of House procedures should be "to secure accuracy in business, economy in time, order, uniformity, and impartiality." The most important change made by the 1880 reforms was in the status of the Rules Committee. It was raised from a select committee, where it had functioned since the beginnings of the House, to a standing committee. The Speaker, who had served as chairman of the select committee since 1858, was likewise made chairman of the permanent committee.

These reforms proved to be some of the most significant alterations ever made in House procedure. The Rules Committee now began to make systematic use of its power to establish rules and regulations governing legislation. It could determine the amount of time that would be allowed for debate on a specific bill, as well as set the number of amendments that could be offered from the House floor. When accepted by a majority of the House—as they usually were, for the sake of efficiency—the time and amendment limitations then controlled the course of the legislation on the House floor and could not be violated.

On paper, the strengthening of the Rules Committee made sense. It helped the House speed up business and avoid long quarrels over important bills. It could be used as a means to overcome the dilatory tactics of determined groups of representatives opposed to certain legislation. But like every reform, the strengthening of the Rules Committee led to new problems its proponents had not foreseen. In this case, it was the abuse of the great power that had now fallen into the hands of the Rules Committee chairman.

Earlier in this chapter, we saw how the House stripped Speaker Joe Cannon of his right to serve as chairman of Rules as part of its effort to destroy Cannon's enormous power and influence. No longer would the Speaker also control the Rules Committee. In his place, the House made arrangements for the appointment of a chairman who would maintain the independence of the committee from undue outside influence. At the same time, however, the House took none of the powers from the chairman who soon came to control the committee in much the same way that Reed and Cannon had controlled the House.

A perceptive student of the period, Chang-wei Chiu, has written that "the power of the chairman of the committee seems to have no limit." The Rules Committee after 1910, he concluded, was guilty of "abuses at which even the Czar Cannon would look with disfavor." The power of the chairman can best be presented by quoting the words of one representative, Philip Campbell (Republican, Kansas), who served in that position. "You can go to hell," he told the committee once when it disagreed with him. "It makes no difference what a majority of you decide. If it meets with my disapproval, it shall not be done. I am the committee. In me repose absolute obstructive powers."

After 1937, the Rules Committee came under the domination of a deeply conservative chairman and was composed of members often equally conservative. It opposed all pieces of progressive legislation favored by many in Congress and by the President. It blocked many economic and social measures it considered too radical and socialistic. As a result, it aroused the wrath of many liberals and became one of their chief targets for reform. Indeed, much of the history of the House of Representatives in the twentieth century can be seen as an attempt to bring the Rules Committee under control, just as the history of the House in the nineteenth century can be seen as a struggle to tame the filibuster and overcome the dilatory tactics that reduced efficiency and wasted time.

III

LIKE THE Speaker and the system of rules and customs, committees date from the earliest period of House history. The idea for committees came from the English House of Commons and the legislatures of the original colonies. Their purpose was to divide the work before the House, so that each representative would not have to be responsible for every bill under consideration. In the early House, committees of three or fewer members were chosen by the Speaker, while larger ones were elected by ballot by the whole House.

At first, most committees were select, which meant that they were drawn up for a short time and dissolved when the reason for their creation was completed. This system, however, quickly proved inadequate because certain areas of House activity—such as tax problems and spending appropriations—needed the kind of expertise that came only with long familiarity with the problems and issues at hand. The move was made from select committees to standing, or permanent, committees. Among the most important of the early standing committees were the Committee on Elections, established 1789, the Interstate and Foreign Commerce Committee, founded in 1795, and the Ways and Means Committee, which dates from 1802.

Between 1809 and 1825, the number of standing committees grew from ten to twenty-eight, while the number of select committees dropped from 350 to 70 by 1815 and then continued to shrink. During the same period, the standing committees acquired the right to report a bill directly to the House (or to refuse to report it, in which case the bill "died in committee"). The adoption of this rule in 1822 showed that the committees had become the chief forums for the initiation of legislation.

Most committees were responsible for the drafting of new bills. They held hearings to gather information, carefully constructed and wrote laws to answer the problem they were considering, and then took the completed bill to the House floor. Very early, however, many committees also took on another function. This was the investigation of government activities to uncover waste, misuse of power, or mismanagement and the questioning of federal officials to see if the laws passed by Congress were being carried out.

Investigations were conducted from the beginning of the House, but became more frequent as time passed. In 1816, Henry Clay, the Speaker of the House, established six committees on expenditures to look into the efficiency and economy of the administration of President James Madison. During the next ten years, these committees and others conducted twenty important inquiries into charges that had been made against a secretary of the treasury, a secretary of war, and the conduct of General Andrew Jackson during the Seminole War in Florida.

The power of the House to investigate the workings of the bureaucracy has frequently aroused the concern of chief executives. George Washington and Thomas Jefferson, as well as later Presidents, have charged that House investigations undermine their authority by giving the legislative branch of government superiority over the executive. This, they claimed, was a violation of the balance of powers created by the Constitution. But complain as they might, Presidents have not been able to bring a halt to investigatory committees. By 1825, according to one journalist of the period, the committees had become "a part of the political machinery of the day. Often the investigations were conducted into legitimate problems." But all too frequently, according to the same journalist, they were held simply to give political advantage to the majority party of the House in upcoming elections, by casting doubt on the honesty and ability of members of the opposing party.

In the years after the Civil War, committees grew in importance. This was in part due to the vast increase in government expenditures caused by the war. Between 1860 and 1865, the annual federal budget grew from $63 million to $1.3 billion—a growth of more than 1,800 percent in five years. Many representatives, appalled by the size of the budget and fearful that the House had lost its control of government spending, began to call for reform.

Taxing and spending had traditionally been the responsibility of the Ways and Means Committee, but now expenditures were moved to two other committees, the Committee on Appropriations and the Banking and Currency Committee. These two committees began to exercise tight control of federal money by bringing an end to wartime monetary practices that had been designed to make money readily available in time of crisis. The work of the Appropriations Committee, charged with the responsibility to use its "whole labor in the restraint of extravagant and illegal appropriations," was especially effective. Between 1871 and 1890, it helped to hold government spending below $300 million for every year but one.

This frugality was largely the result of the "tight purse" policies of Appropriations Committee chairman, Samuel Randall, later Speaker of the House. By saying no to many projects he considered to be of questionable value, Randall was able to hold spending at a minimum, but at a cost to himself and his committee. Angered by his refusal to approve many "pork barrel" schemes,* members of the House stripped Appropriations of its authority over expenditures for rivers and harbors in 1877. By 1885, the power to control spending in other areas, including agriculture, the army and navy, consular and diplomatic affairs, post office and post roads, Indian affairs, and the military academy, were likewise taken from the committee, leaving it in charge of less than half of the federal expenditures.

* *Pork barrel* is American slang for a government appropriation that supplies funds for local improvements designed to win the approval of a legislator's constituents and thereby gain their votes. Pork barrel projects have included new post offices, federal buildings, roads, dams, and so on.

As the power to spend passed from the Appropriations Committee, it moved to other committees and to other committee chairmen. Indeed, the attack on Randall's authority and "tight purse" policies was led by senior members of the House who believed that Randall's use of power had undermined their own prestige and influence. But the senior members did not stand alone. They were joined by young as well as older representatives, by Republicans as well as Democrats.

The revolt against the Appropriations Committee emphasized the rivalries and struggle for power that have characterized much of the history of the modern House. It likewise paved the way for the extreme decentralization of power that led to what has been called "government by committee." Mary Parker Follett, a perceptive observer of the House and Senate, wrote at the time that "Congress no longer exercises its lawful function of lawmaking; that has gone to the committees as completely as in England it has passed to the Cabinet."

The young Woodrow Wilson, then a graduate student at the Johns Hopkins University and later President of the United States, put it another way. In his book *Congressional Government*, Wilson wrote that power in the House was distributed among "forty-seven seignories, in each of which a standing committee is the court-baron and its chairman lord-proprietor." This has led to a situation, Wilson concluded, where "chairman fights against chairman" and where the best interests of democratic government are not served.

The growth of committee autonomy helped to emphasize two traits that had long been part of House custom: secrecy and seniority. The Constitution required that the House publish a journal of its activities during general sessions, but this was not applied to committees. Committee meetings, more often than not, were held in closed session, with no record made for public consumption. This gave many representatives the chance to speak their minds without condemnation, but it also led to suspicion that the representatives had something to hide: why else should they conduct their most important business in private? With the expansion of committee power, the practice of secrecy grew, so that in the twentieth century, one of the harshest criticisms of the House has been its refusal to "go public."

The custom of seniority has likewise been used by the House since very early in its history. It seemed natural as well as wise to appoint men of long experience to key positions. In the nineteenth century, however, seniority was practiced only haphazardly and inconsistently. In our own century, it became a habit the House rarely deviated from. The result was a House dominated by old men who happened to chair important committees. Frequently these men were in their late seventies or eighties, suspicious of new ideas and always jealous custodians of their own authority. But the strongest charge that could be brought against seniority was not age; it was regionalism. Certain sections of the country, like the South, tended to reelect their representatives more regularly than other sections. Hence those regions enjoyed the greatest influence in the House, while the others had less influence.

But there was also a more positive side to the practice of seniority. As the importance of committees grew, so too did the number of representatives who made the House their career and who chose to become specialists and experts in different areas of legislation. The early House had been characterized by a frequent turnover in membership and a marked lack of professionalism. The House of the twentieth century, by comparison, has enjoyed the service of men and women who have devoted their lives to its work and whose expertise in their areas of specialization has often been striking.

After 1910, the two most obvious features of House practice

and proceedings were their complexity and the decentralization of authority. Strong, centralized leadership had been rejected in favor of a Speaker whose powers were carefully limited by custom. The enormous, complicated body of rules—which few representatives understood—served to bring order and harmony to the House but at the same time were exploited by powerful and influential members for their own purposes. Genuine authority was divided among the committee chairmen, who controlled the legislative process with an iron hand.

Complexity and decentralization are not necessarily faults and imperfections, but they can be, and were, in the case of the House of Representatives in this century. They helped to give the House a rigidity and immobility that made it difficult to respond to new problems and situations. As the nation faced the immense social, economic, and political problems raised by the world wars, the Great Depression, and other important crises, the House came more and more to rely on the guidance and help of the President and executive bureaucracy, and less on its own initiative.

But the situation was not hopeless. Throughout its history, the House had frequently proved its ability to change with changing circumstances. Rules had been altered to improve the flow of business, the function of leadership had been changed, even the power of committees had been modified. It was this ability to change, as we shall see, that helped the House adjust to the problems raised by the twentieth century and to establish new rules and practices to govern its proceedings.

CHAPTER FOUR

THE SENATE IN PRACTICE

The Senate of the United States is "the most remarkable of all the inventions of modern politics"—William Gladstone, PRIME MINISTER OF GREAT BRITAIN

THE SENATE envisioned by the Founding Fathers was primarily a deliberative body composed of the best educated, most experienced and accomplished men the nation had to offer. Its members would debate affairs of state, advise the President, and provide, in the words of Edmund Randolph of Virginia, a curb against the "turbulence and follies of democracy." The Senate, where every state was equally represented, fulfilled the "federal" ideal of government, while the House, whose membership was based on population, fulfilled the "national" ideal. Senators were to be chosen by the state legislatures, in the belief that the legislatures would choose only the most able and responsible men. This kept the Senate once removed from the "people" and less likely to be swayed by the passions of the moment.

The small size of the Senate also made it very different from the House. There were two senators from each state; this meant that the first Senate of 1789 consisted of only twenty-two men.* Even today, the Senate, with one hundred members, is far smaller than the 435-member House. This smallness has helped to give each senator a sense of individuality and importance impossible to the members of the other body. Senators, said Daniel Webster, who served in both the House and Senate, acknowledge no master and accept no dictation. They belong, he added, to an association of "equals, of men of individual honor and personal character, and of absolute independence."

But perhaps the most striking difference between the House and Senate is the Senate's tradition of "unlimited debate." Unlimited debate became the most prized possession of the upper house, and it was a possession relinquished only in times of national crisis or when the need for action overrode the need for discussion and deliberation. The right to debate at length—largely abandoned by the House because of the great number of representatives—gave individual senators the chance to emerge as the leaders of national causes or movements and become the symbols for those who thought as they did. The right of debate likewise frequently made senators the most vocal opponents of the President and his policies.

This trait irked the young Woodrow Wilson, who wrote in his book *Congressional Government* in 1885 that "the Senate is merely a body of individual critics" without purpose and direction. But the individuality of the Senate and its right to debate have been attractive to many others, including members of the House of Representatives. Since the earliest Congress, many representatives have jumped at the opportunity to move on to the Senate, which then benefited from their experience. The superiority of the Senate, Senator Thomas Hart Benton observed in 1825, derives from the fact that it is composed of "the pick of the House of Repre-

* When the first Senate met, two states had not yet ratified the Constitution and therefore had not elected senators.

sentatives, and thereby gains doubly—by brilliant accession to itself and abstraction from the other."

The virtue of the Senate was recognized by foreign observers who came to the United States to study the American government and its workings. Alexis de Tocqueville, the French historian and political philosopher, described the Senate of the 1830s as a place where "scarcely an individual is to be found . . . who does not recall the idea of an active and illustrious career." The Senate, he observed, "is composed of eloquent advocates, distinguished generals, wise magistrates, and statesmen of note, whose language would, at all times, do honor to the most remarkable parliamentary debates of Europe." James Bryce, an English ambassador to the United States, called the Senate "the masterpiece of the constitution makers, and William Gladstone, in the passage quoted at the opening of this chapter, said it was a "most remarkable" invention. For these men, the Senate was the crowning glory of the American system of government.

I

The Senate was an original creation of the Founding Fathers. It was modeled on no existing legislature, nor did it derive from one in the past. The House of Representatives could look to the House of Commons, the lower house of the English Parliament, but the Senate could not pattern itself on the House of Lords without arousing suspicion and opposition. The privileged and titled nobility sat in the House of Lords and all privilege and noble status had been outlawed in the United States.

Without a model to pattern itself upon, the Senate turned to practice and experience to determine the extent and nature of its powers and authority. Three important questions seemed to deserve an answer. What was the Senate's relationship to the President and the executive branch? What was its relationship to the House of Representatives, the other half of Congress? And what was its relationship to the states and to the state legislatures that were responsible for the election of senators? The last question has been answered successfully, but the other two continue to raise problems and may never be solved to everyone's satisfaction.

The question of the relationship between the Senate and the President is particularly touchy. The Constitution gives the President the authority to make treaties and appoint many government officials, but it also requires that he share this power with the Senate. To become law, treaties must be approved by two-thirds of the Senate, whereas presidential appointments need a simple majority to be confirmed. But where does presidential authority end and the authority of the Senate begin? By voting against treaties and appointments, a determined Senate can undermine the authority of a President and make havoc of his policies and administration. This has happened several times in our history. The only recourse has been a strong President able to use the power and influence of his office to sway the Senate in his favor.

The first major confrontation between a President and the Senate occurred during the administration of Andrew Jackson. Jackson was a strong, vigorous President who was able to dominate the House of Representatives but found himself opposed in the Senate by a number of senators who were members of the Whig party. Jackson, a Democrat, supported the supremacy of the executive branch; the Whigs, under the leadership of Senator Henry Clay, were advocates of legislative supremacy. The Whigs did not hesitate to attack the policies of the President—to whom they gave the name "King Andrew"—and to denounce his methods of leadership.

Several issues were disputed between Jackson and the Whigs, but the most important was the Bank of the United States. Jackson opposed the bank, because he believed it served only the interests of the wealthy, and used his authority as President to remove all federal deposits from it. The Whigs, who supported the bank, took the position that Jackson had exceeded his powers and had acted dictatorially in failing to consult the Congress about his removal of the deposits. The Senate launched an investigation into the President's actions and demanded to see his communications with his cabinet officers on the issue of the bank. But Jackson ignored the demands and refused to hand over the information.

The stage was set for a confrontation between the President and the Senate. In 1834, Henry Clay pushed through the Senate a bill of censure that charged "that the President, in the late executive proceedings in relation to the public revenue, has assumed upon himself authority and power not conferred by the Constitution and laws and in derogation of both." The President replied by saying that the charges amounted to an impeachment, and since the House of Representatives had the sole power to initiate impeachment proceedings, the Senate was at fault when it issued the censure.

Jackson's friends in the Senate then began a campaign to remove the censure from the Senate *Journal*. Several state legislatures, friendly to the President's aims, instructed their senators to support Jackson; other legislatures simply removed anti-Jackson senators from office. The result was that by 1837, Jacksonian Democrats were in a majority, and the Senate voted twenty-four to nineteen to remove the censure. In a dramatic ceremony, the journal of the year 1834 was brought into the Senate chamber where the secretary of the Senate wrote in bold letters across the censure statement: "Expunged by order of the Senate, the 16th day of January, in the year of our Lord 1837."

Jackson had won in his confrontation with the Senate, but later Presidents were not to be so fortunate. A few years later, the Senate and a new President, John Tyler, once again clashed over the question of authority. Henry Clay hoped the Senate could dominate the new President and force him to accept its legislative program, but Tyler proved intransigent. He vetoed bills passed by the Congress and refused to acknowledge Clay's leadership. The Senate, in turn, rejected many of Tyler's nominations for public office, including four appointments to cabinet posts. When Tyler left the presidency in 1845, its powers were in disarray and the power of the Senate was on the rise.

Other confrontations between the chief executive and the Senate have followed the patterns set by the Jackson and Tyler episodes. Strong Presidents tend to dominate the Congress, but in doing so arouse deep resentment and antipathy. This resentment and antipathy, in turn, lead Congress to challenge the President and to reassert its claims to be an equal partner in the American system of government.* There seems to be no simple solution to this dilemma and no way to strike a balance that will endure between the two branches. The relationship between the President and the Senate is continual debate that must be settled anew with every generation.

The second question asked at the beginning of this section concerned the relationship of the Senate and the House of Representatives. This question, too, involved the problem of power and influence. Were the two houses, for instance, fully equal associates in the national legislature and, if so, how was this equality to be worked out? The chief difficulty from the Senate's point of

* Similar confrontations between the President and the Senate have arisen during the administrations of Abraham Lincoln and Andrew Johnson, Woodrow Wilson, Franklin Roosevelt, and Richard Nixon. Lincoln succeeded in dominating Congress during the Civil War, but his successor, Johnson, was impeached by the House and came within one vote in the Senate of removal from office. Wilson saw his pet project, the League of Nations, defeated by a Senate long disenchanted with his presidency. Roosevelt dominated Congress during his first term, but afterwards faced a restless and rebellious Senate. Nixon resigned rather than face impeachment for criminal activity by a Congress deeply critical of his behavior as President.

view was the issue of appropriations, which is the power to decide how federal money is to be spent.

The final draft of the Constitution explicitly granted the House of Representatives the sole authority to originate "all bills for raising revenue," but did not grant a similar power over appropriations. An earlier draft of the Constitution, however, had said that "all bills for raising and appropriating money . . . shall originate in the House" and on the basis of this early consideration, the House of Representatives assumed the right to control spending, as well as taxation. The early Senate recognized this right, and soon the practice became fixed by custom and tradition.

But the problem was not completely settled. From time to time, jurisdictional disputes would flare up in which the House would protest that the Senate had overstepped its authority and the Senate would counter with charges that the House controlled spending too thoroughly and left too little for the Senate to do in the appropriations process. These disputes created a rift between the two houses and led to a feud in 1962 that revealed how deep the disagreement had become.

The feud began when the House Appropriations Committee, irked by what it regarded as the "superior" behavior of the Senate, refused to go over to the Senate side of the Capitol for a meeting with the Senate Appropriations Committee. The meetings and their location in the Senate wing had been a regular occurrence for many years, but now the House Committee refused to comply. Instead, it demanded that the Senate come to the House wing or find some neutral area in which to hold the joint conference.

The dispute over location soon grew into a far larger disagreement. The House held up consideration of all government spending programs until the Senate clarified the position it expected to play in the appropriations process. Did the Senate expect to initiate its own appropriations bills? Did it expect to be able to add new funds to bills already passed by the House for projects the House had not considered or had considered and rejected? The questions, to which the House expected an answer of "no," tied up Congress for several months.

In order to provide funds for federal agencies that were running out of money while Congress debated, the Senate passed a "continuing resolution" designed to make money available until the final budget was drawn up. But the House protested this action, claiming that it was an infringement of its "immemorial" right to originate all revenue and spending bills. The Senate replied with a resolution that said the clear language of the Constitution permitted it to originate any legislation that did not involve "raising revenue." For a while, the feud remained a standoff, but finally, a truce was reached and Congress resumed its regular business. The truce, however, settled none of the problems at issue between the two houses, and it was left to the House and Senate of a decade later to work out a new compromise, which, in time, may prove to have solved the argument over appropriations.

The third question that opened this section involved the relationship of the Senate to the states and state legislatures. At issue here were problems that may not be immediately apparent. Early senators had regarded themselves as ambassadors from the states they represented and had, on occasion, accepted instruction from the state legislatures that elected them to office. This was truer of senators from southern states than it was of senators from the North.

As time passed, however, this practice began to fade. With the growth of political parties, senators accepted party discipline and loyalty as sufficient guidelines for the positions they took on important issues. But the question of the Senate's allegiance remained in the public mind. By the end of the nineteenth century and the appearance of the progressive movement with its demands for greater democracy and honesty in government, the Senate had become a very hot issue. On both counts—democracy and honesty—the Senate was vulnerable. Its election by the state legislatures was regarded as proof that it was isolated from the average citizen, who had very little or no say in the selection of his senators. And its isolation from and unresponsiveness to the needs of the average citizen led to the suspicion that the Senate was in the pay of the nation's wealthy financiers and commercial interests, to whom it owed its allegiance.

Calls for the direct election of senators as a means of making them subject to the will of the people had been made from time to time in the nineteenth century, but by the end of the century they had become commonplace. To all of them, the Senate turned a deaf ear. The powerful Committee on Privileges and Elections refused to bring such suggestions before the Senate or to consider them seriously. Pressure for change, however, became enormous and came from a variety of sources including public petitions, referenda, state governments, and even the House of Representatives, which voted to urge the Senate to accept the direct election of senators.

The final stage in the movement was reached when several states threatened to call a constitutional convention to amend the Constitution. Many senators, even those who opposed direct election, feared that a constitutional convention would prove a disaster. It might not stop at the direct election of senators, but alter other sections as well, leading to a basic change in the American form of government. All previous amendments to the Constitution had originated in Congress, and the Senate wanted to reserve this power to itself and the House.

In 1911, a bill prescribing the direct election of senators came up for its first vote in the Senate and failed. The next year, however, it passed and in 1913, after ratification by three-fourths of the states, it became the Seventeenth Amendment to the Constitution. The question of the relationship of the Senate to the states had finally been settled in favor of the people. By 1919, the last senators elected by the state legislatures had left office and the first Senate, completely chosen by direct election, had assembled in Washington.

The one characteristic of the Senate that can be gleaned from this discussion of its evolving relationship with the President, the House, and the states is the Senate's capacity for change. When challenged by the power of a strong President, the Senate has, in turn, risen to the occasion and brought Presidents low. When jurisdictional disputes with the House have emerged, compromises have been reached to bring order and harmony. And, as we have seen, the Senate altered the method of election of its own members. This capacity for change should not be overemphasized—after all, direct election was passed only after great pressure had been brought to bear on the upper house—but it has nevertheless served the Senate well and has helped it adapt to changing circumstances and new problems.

II

THE CONSTITUTION answered the problem of Senate leadership by appointing the Vice-President to sit as president of the Senate. Indeed, other than his responsibility to succeed to the presidency upon the death of the President, this was the only service the Vice-President performed for his government. Even this role, however, presented complications. Since the Vice-President was imposed on the Senate from the outside and not elected by its members, he could not expect to be regarded as a genuine leader of that body. John Adams, the first Vice-President, solved this dilemma by serving simply as a presiding officer and making little effort to guide or control Senate activity. For the most part, his precedent has been followed by his successors.

The Constitution also provided for a second Senate officer, which it called the president pro tempore, from the Latin for "temporary" or "for the time being." The president pro tempore was to be elected by the Senate and was expected to preside in the absence of the Vice-President. By the very nature of his office, however, the president pro tempore could not be expected to emerge as a major Senate leader. In the early Senate, presidents pro tempore tended to serve for short periods of time—fifteen different senators held the position during the first twelve years of Senate history—and were unable to develop the power and authority an important leader must have.

With the Vice-President and the president pro tempore out of the question, actual leadership in the Senate soon passed to individual senators who stood out because of their talents and abilities. During the first half of the nineteenth century, several of these figures were among the most outstanding men who have sat in the Senate. These include figures we have already mentioned, like Henry Clay, Daniel Webster, and John Calhoun, but the list also comprised Sam Houston (Democrat, Texas), William Seward (Republican, New York), Jefferson Davis (Democrat, Mississippi), Stephen Douglas (Democrat, Illinois), and others. Under their leadership, the power of the Senate often dominated the federal government, outshining both the House of Representatives and the President.

After the Civil War, however, the quality of Senate leadership underwent a marked decline. The Senate was now filled with men called "party bosses," who had risen to power through their work in the political party machines of their home states. Their loyalty was based on party membership, to which they believed they owed everything, and they resisted political pressure that came from outside their group of friends, associates, and fellow party members. The most famous of their number were Mark Hanna (Republican, Ohio), Roscoe Conkling (Republican, New York),

Matthew Quay (Republican, Pennsylvania), and James G. Blaine.* They were men who achieved many things, such as the building of railroads and the expansion of the country's industrial and commercial life, but they were also men who brought the reputation of the Senate to an all-time low. Their intimate connection with wealthy business interests led the public to suspect corruption and bribery—and rightly so in many cases.†

A new method of Senate leadership began to take form toward the end of the century. The nucleus of the reform was a group of Republican senators, known as the Philosophy Club, that met regularly for a game of poker at the home of Senator Joseph McClellan of Michigan. When one of their number, William Allison of Iowa, was chosen head of the Republican caucus in 1897, the group moved to take control of the party and of the Senate. "Both in the committees and in the offices," Allison said, "we should use the machinery for our own benefit and not let other men have it."

Allison sought complete domination of the Senate, just as Speaker Reed had controlled the House of Representatives after 1890. Allison took charge of the Republican Steering Committee and filled it with other members of the Philosophy Club. He then used the Steering Committee to arrange the order of business in the Senate and manage proceedings on the floor. Allison also took control of the Republican Committee on Committees, which was responsible for the appointment of Republican senators to

* These men were all Republicans, but that does not mean that the Democratic party of the period was free of party bosses or corruption. After the Civil War, the Republicans dominated the Senate for many years, and therefore the most powerful men in the Senate at that time tended to be Republicans.

† These men recognized their deficiencies. Once, when Blaine was running for President and Conkling was asked to campaign for him, Conkling refused, saying, "I don't engage in criminal practice."

committee positions, and employed his authority to fill committee vacancies with senators loyal to him. The Senate that Allison helped to create was one where party discipline was paramount and where individual senators gained power and influence by going along with the party leadership. It was also a more tightly run and better managed Senate than had existed earlier.

The leadership exerted by Allison, however, and by his friends, such as Nelson Aldrich (Republican, Rhode Island), was unofficial. Allison was chairman of the Republican caucus, and Aldrich was chairman of the Senate Finance Committee. They both exerted far more authority than these posts would warrant, and when they left the Senate, the authority left with them. No other senator had accumulated the prestige and influence they had accumulated—and that they were willing to exercise—and after them party discipline threatened to diminish.

Obviously, the one solution was to create a single, official position to be occupied by a senator who could serve as spokesman for his party. This the Democrats proceeded to do in 1911 with the election of a leader who was both floor leader for his party and chairman of the party caucus.* After the elections of 1912, when the Democrats gained control of the Senate, their leader was known as the majority leader, while the Republicans, now in the minority, chose a senator to serve as their minority leader. Soon afterward, both parties elected majority and minority whips to assist the party leaders. To this day, the majority and minority leaders are recognized as the spokesmen for their parties in the Senate. A few senators may surpass them in fame and prestige, but none has more control over the day-to-day business of the Senate.

* Around this time, the word *conference* frequently was substituted for *caucus*. Today, for instance, the Republicans in the House are said to hold a conference rather than caucus. Usage, however, is uneven, and the press often uses both words to mean the same thing.

III

THE HISTORY of rules in the Senate is very different from the history of rules in the House of Representatives. There are several reasons why this should be so. The small size and more intimate character of the Senate has meant that its rules could be simple and few in number compared with the complex and numerous rules of the House. Moreover, the longer term enjoyed by the senator—six years compared to the two-year tenure of the representative—has allowed the average senator to have a more relaxed and informal attitude toward rules and regulations. "Rules are never observed in this body," said Senator John Ingalls (Republican, Kansas) in 1876. "They are only made to be broken. We are a law unto ourselves." No member of the House of Representatives, with its obsession with form and procedure, could have made this statement. From the beginning, House rules have stressed the need for action and good organization to facilitate legislation, whereas those of the Senate have emphasized time for deliberation, debate, and the expression of opinions from individual senators.

The first Senate adopted only twenty rules to govern its behavior, but these soon proved inadequate. They were amended during Thomas Jefferson's term as Vice-President and president of the Senate (1797–1801) to include his *Manual of Parliamentary Procedure*, which he had drawn up for his own use, in order, he said, to be able to refer "to some known system of rules." But Senate rules have never numbered very many. By 1806, they had grown to forty, which were revised somewhat in 1820 and 1828. The fifty-three rules the Senate adopted in 1869 were a rare exception and reflected the strains of the Civil War on the government. By 1884, they were back down again to forty.

Some historians have concluded that the small number of Senate rules explains why movements for reform have played so small a part in the life of the Senate compared to that of the House of Representatives. According to this theory, the Senate has chosen to live without an excessive number of rules or to ignore them if they prove to be restrictive and too limiting. The House, on the other hand, has tended to accumulate rules without end, in the name of greater order and efficiency, until a point is reached where reform is necessary.

One area of Senate activity, however, has raised major difficulties and led to demands for change, similar to the reform movements in the House. This is the practice of filibuster. The word *filibuster* comes from the Spanish word for "freebooter," or "pirate." It refers to the seizure of the Senate floor by a group of senators in order to bring business to a halt and stop the passage of legislation they oppose. In the House of Representatives, filibustering was brought under control by a series of strict rules and is now a rare occurrence. But in the Senate, with its tradition of "unlimited debate," filibustering has proved to be a considerable hindrance to Senate activity.

Filibustering can take several forms. Dissident senators can exploit parliamentary tactics to stall business and create havoc. They can call for postponements or for adjournment, again and again, and ask for a roll-call vote on each motion. Or they can take advantage of special committee regulations to stop the consideration of bills. Senator Albert Beveridge (Republican, Indiana), for instance, hid for days in Washington and then went to Atlantic City, New Jersey, because he opposed a bill that would give statehood to New Mexico and Arizona. Because he was chairman of the Territories Committee, which was in charge of the bill, his presence in the Senate chamber was necessary before it could be brought to a vote; without him, no vote could be taken. The bill was finally dropped so that other business could be taken up. The most familiar type of filibuster, however, is the marathon speech where one senator holds the floor for hours, yielding it only to other senators who share his views. Filibustering senators have read endlessly from the Bible, from Shakespeare, or have spoken only on the issue at hand. In any case, the result has been the same: boredom for those senators who remain in the Senate chamber and the delay of important legislation.

Filibustering first came into prominence in the 1840s. In 1841, a group of senators held up Senate business for ten days to stop a bill that would remove the Senate printers. Later the same year, another group filibustered for two weeks against a bill that called for the reestablishment of the Bank of the United States, the same issue that had divided the Senate and the President during the administration of Andrew Jackson. Henry Clay, who supported the bill, threatened to impose a gag rule on the opponents—a threat he was never able to carry out. The bill finally passed the Senate, only to be vetoed by the President. Clay's failure to obtain a gag rule against the dissidents was indicative of the attitude of the Senate. Although a majority of senators supported the bank, they did not want to impose a limitation on debate that might someday be used against them.

The filibuster became a more frequent occurrence in the years after the Civil War. By the 1880s and 1890s it had assumed the character of a habit. In 1881, Senate Democrats stopped Senate activity for almost two months and forced the resignations of two prominent Republican senators. In 1890, a force bill—one that would have required federal supervision of polling places in order to prevent the exclusion of black voters—was held up for seven weeks by southern senators who opposed it. During this filibuster, Senator C. J. Faulkner (Democrat, West Virginia) held the floor for eleven and a half hours.

A filibuster of more than two months against the Silver Purchase Act of 1893 aroused a great deal of antipathy among the public and press, who began to call for reform of Senate procedure. They were seconded by many in the Senate. Said Henry Cabot Lodge (Republican, Massachusetts), "As it is, there must be a change, for the delays which now take place are discrediting the Senate. A body which cannot govern itself will not long hold the respect of the people who have chosen it to govern the country." This was the heyday, wrote historian Franklin Burdette, "of brazen and unblushing aggressors. The power of the Senate lay not in votes but in sturdy tongues and iron wills. The premium rested not upon ability and statesmanship but upon effrontery and audacity."

In spite of the dissatisfaction with the excesses of filibustering, reforms were slow in coming. During the pressures of the Civil War, the Senate voted to limit debate to five minutes, but this stipulation covered only subjects related to the war and considered in secret session. In 1870, a new rule was adopted that helped to facilitate the flow of business. Named for its sponsor, Senator Henry Anthony (Republican, Rhode Island), the Anthony Rule allowed for a daily consideration of routine bills by setting aside the period from the conclusion of the morning's business until the two o'clock afternoon session for this purpose. The Anthony Rule did not stop filibustering, but it did assure that less important bills would be brought before the Senate and not be pushed aside by debate on major bills.

Champion filibusterers could still hold the Senate at bay for days. In 1903, Senator Benjamin "Pitchfork Ben" Tillman (Democrat, South Carolina) threatened to read the Senate all of Lord Byron's long poem "Childe Harold" unless it agreed to pay back to his home state a claim that dated from the Civil War. In 1908, Robert La Follette held the floor for eighteen hours and twenty-three minutes during a bitterly contested debate on an emergency currency measure—a filibustering record that endured for thirty years. Senate leaders denounced Tillman's actions as "legislative blackmail" and criticized La Follette for holding up important business, but both men defended their tactics as the only means available to assure that minority opinions were heard in the Senate and not drowned by the power of the majority.

La Follette's filibuster of 1908 led to new Senate rulings that attempted to curb obstruction, but these lacked serious bite. It took two more major filibusters, one in 1915 and another in 1917, to force the Senate into action. The 1917 filibuster was one of the most dramatic and spectacular in Senate history. President Wilson, fearful that America was about to be drawn into World War I against Germany, asked Congress for authority to arm American merchant ships. The President was thinking in terms of "armed neutrality"—a situation where the nation prepares for war, but stops short of entry.

The vast majority of the Senate supported Wilson, but eleven senators opposed him and were able to stop consideration of the bill during the last days of that session of Congress. Seventy-five senators out of ninety-six signed a statement, which was entered in the Senate record and which said that the Senate favored the measure and "would pass it, if a vote could be had." But a vote could not be taken. On the last day of the session, when La Follette, who had led the filibuster, rose to speak, he was himself filibustered by Democrats angered by his refusal to support the bill.

President Wilson was perhaps angriest of all. "The Senate of the United States," he declared, "is the only legislative body in the world which cannot act when its majority is ready for action. A little group of willful men"—a reference to the eleven filibusterers—"representing no opinion but their own, have rendered the great government of the United States helpless and contemptible." Wilson then moved to call the Senate into a special session and asked that it change its rules to "save the country from disaster." The mood of the country supported the President.

In the special session that followed, the Senate leaders of both parties worked together to draw up what has come to be known as Rule 22, the Senate's first cloture rule that provided a means to bring an end to a filibuster. Rule 22 allowed for limitation of debate on any pending measure, by a vote of two-thirds of the senators present and voting, two days after a cloture motion had been presented by sixteen senators. After a successful vote, debate was limited to one hour for each senator on the bill itself and on all amendments or motions related to it. No new amendments to the bill could be offered unless the Senate agreed to them by unanimous consent. Amendments that were not related to the business at hand or that were designed to delay action were to be considered out of order.

The cloture rule gave the Senate its first means to limit debate and control filibustering. In practice, however, the rule proved difficult to carry out. The two-thirds majority needed to effect cloture meant that sixty-four out of ninety-six senators had to favor the motion. To get sixty-four senators to agree on any one measure was a formidable task. During the next fifteen years, the Senate invoked cloture on eleven occasions, only four of which were successful in limiting debate and bringing the filibuster to an end. But the cloture rule was a beginning, and steps would later be taken to strengthen its power over filibusterers.

IV

The first Senate committees were small ad hoc committees chosen to consider specific issues and then disbanded when their business was completed. This system was in keeping with the small size of the Senate, its intimate atmosphere, and its comparatively light workload, which on occasion allowed an early adjournment of daily sessions so that the senators could visit the House of Representatives to hear the more lively debates there. The small workload also made it possible for every senator to keep close watch on the work of each committee, even when he did not serve on that committee.

The change to standing, or permanent, committees came gradually. Only four were established during the first twenty-five years of the Senate. By 1816, however, the number of ad hoc committees had grown to almost one hundred, well over twice the number of senators who served in the Senate at that time. Since the Senate had to appoint each committee and set its jurisdiction, much time and effort were lost that could be spent on more important issues. Following the pattern already established by the House, the Senate responded to this dilemma by creating eleven new standing committees. They included committees on Commerce and Manufactures, Military Affairs, Finance, the Judiciary, and Foreign Relations. Ad hoc committees had usually consisted of three members; the new permanent committees were given five members.

The early Senate had chosen committee members by ballot so that the whole body was involved in the selection process. In 1823, this was changed to allow the presiding officer to appoint committees in order to save time. The Senate had expected this authority to be exercised by the president pro tempore, who was himself a senator. But in 1825 and 1826, Vice-President John Calhoun, acting in his position of president of the Senate, usurped the power and began to abuse it by appointing his supporters to important committees. The Senate responded in 1828 by specifically granting the authority to name committees to the president pro tempore.

In 1833, however, the Senate returned to ballot to select committees and in 1846 overhauled the system once again to establish the method of committee selection it has followed to the present day. The change came suddenly in December, 1846, as the Senate followed its regular routine and balloted for committee appointments. Halfway through the balloting, the rule was suspended and the Senate proceeded to vote on a list of committee nominations drawn up by representatives from the majority and minority parties. Since that time, committee appointments have been controlled by the political parties and routinely accepted by the Senate as a whole.

The new system strengthened the power of political parties in the Senate and paved the way for the importance party discipline and loyalty were to play by the end of the century. At the same time, it increased the significance of seniority as a means to achieve status and prestige. In earlier years, the Senate had often followed the principle of seniority in making committee appointments, but with the advent of party lists it became a pattern rigidly adhered to, with very few exceptions. Seniority helped to contribute to stability and harmony in the Senate by providing an orderly way for individual senators to rise to power. But it also had its faults. In 1859, one northern senator called it an "intolerably bad" practice that gave senators from the slave-holding states of the South "the chairmanship of every single committee that controls the public business of this government. There is not one exception." *

Party control of committee appointments was likewise in part responsible for the rapid growth in the number of standing committees after the Civil War. The twenty-five standing committees

* The same criticism could have been made eighty years later, in 1940 and 1950. Southern senators still controlled many of the major committees.

in existence in 1853 became the forty-two of 1889 and seventy-four in 1913. Many of these new committees were the natural outcome of the growing amount of business the Senate had to deal with. But there were other, less acceptable reasons for the expansion of the committee system. Some committees were kept around long after the need for them had disappeared in order to increase the number of chairmanships available for party leaders to bestow on hopeful and loyal senators. Other committees were created for this purpose. Moreover, committee chairmanships provided a means to award senators with additional office space and badly needed clerical assistance they would otherwise not have. Since there were seventy-four chairmanships to give away by 1913, and only ninety-six senators, party leaders had a large "treasure chest" that could be used to instill party discipline.

In 1921, the Senate, spurred on by its Republican majority, began to overhaul the committee system. The seventy-four committees were reduced to thirty-four, a reduction by more than half and a comment on how few of the committees were actually essential to Senate business. The practice of seniority, however, was left intact. Republicans strengthened their hold on committees by increasing the number of members from the majority party who sat on each committee. The thirty-four committees that emerged from the revision were, like the committees in the House of Representatives, centers of power and prestige.

From its beginnings through the first half of the twentieth century, the Senate had changed from an intimate body of twenty-two to a club of one hundred. The decorum and informality that characterized its early years had been largely replaced by an emphasis on party politics, the accumulation of power through seniority, and a system that relied on committees to get legislation prepared and passed. Criticisms of Senate practice had led to the direct election of senators and to the cloture rule of 1917, which was the first major attempt to limit filibustering. The Senate still had problems, however, and it too, like the House, would face a crisis in the mid-twentieth century that would lead to change and reform. It is now time to look at that crisis.

CHAPTER FIVE

CONGRESS IN CRISIS

The role of Congress "has come to be that of a sometimes querulous but essentially kindly uncle who complains while furiously puffing on his pipe but who finally, as everyone expects, gives in and hands over the allowance, grants the permission, or raises his hand in blessing, and then returns to his rocking chair for another year of somnolence broken only by an occasional glance down the avenue and a muttered doubt as to whether he had done the right thing"—Representative Carl Vinson in 1973, after serving forty-nine years in Congress.

BEGINNING WITH the 1930s, Congress has faced a crisis brought on by two developments. The powers and authority of the President have expanded enormously, leaving the House of Representatives and the Senate a poor second in influence and prestige in the workings of the federal government. At the same time, the Congress has failed to change with the times and adopt new practices to meet new problems. As a result, critics in journalism, in the field of political science, and in other areas of government expertise have frequently accused the House and Senate of being "insulated" from public opinion, "closed" to innovation, and "largely unresponsive" to the needs of the nation.

The growth of the presidency and the decline of Congress are related. As more and more Americans came to regard the President as the natural leader of the country in difficult times, they increasingly looked upon Congress as a group of old, cantankerous men bent on thwarting the power of the President and on achieving their own selfish ends. The President was powerful, swift to act in times of crisis, and close to the people. Congress was ingrained in tradition and the prisoner of outmoded custom; it was slow, lethargic, and incapable of facing the complex problems of the modern world.

Partly responsible for the popularity of the President and the decline of congressional prestige was the electronic revolution of the twentieth century and the rapid expansion of media coverage of every facet of governmental activity. In this climate, the President prospered. He was a single, readily identifiable figure who could manipulate radio and later television for his own purposes and help mold public opinion. Congress, on the other hand, was made up of 535 different voices and presented a confused and bewildering impression on the mind of the public. In the age of electronic media, a President could quickly become a hero or a scoundrel, whereas a representative or senator might struggle for years before his name and face became familiar to the nation.

Many of the Presidents of recent years have been the creators of what the noted historian Arthur Schlesinger, Jr., has called "the imperial presidency." These Presidents have included Franklin Roosevelt, Harry Truman, Dwight Eisenhower, John Kennedy, Lyndon Johnson, and Richard Nixon. Responding to genuinely grave situations, Schlesinger notes, these men expanded the powers of the presidency to "imperial" proportions to help the nation meet the problems it faced. In time, however, the power they possessed became excessive and undermined the constitutional balance of powers between the executive and legislative branches of government. This was the crisis Congress faced under the imperial presidency: to find a way to restore the House and Senate to their original partnership with the President and reassert the rights and privileges the Constitution had given them.

I

THE IMPERIAL presidency was born during the period of national emergency and hardship known as the Great Depression. The collapse of the New York stock market in October, 1929, was followed by the most severe economic downturn in America's history. Millions were to lose their jobs, their life savings, and their property. The 1920s, which had been an era of comparative affluence and well-being for many, were followed by years of hunger, privation, and lowered standards of living. To this crisis, Congress and the President, Herbert Hoover, seemed to have no meaningful solution.

In the elections of 1931, the Republicans began to lose the majorities in Congress that they had enjoyed for more than a decade. But it was not until 1933, when the new Democratic President, Franklin Roosevelt, replaced Hoover, that the spirit of innovation began to seize Washington. It was not so much that Roosevelt had the answers that would solve the country's problems—these problems were too serious and extraordinary for one man or set of ideas to solve. It was simply that Roosevelt, who was immensely popular and possessed extraordinary leadership qualities, was willing to take control and to act. Congress, uncertain how to meet the depression, capitulated to the man who had a program—the President.

In his first inaugural address, Roosevelt offered to work with Congress. "In the event the national emergency is still critical," he said, "I shall not evade the clear course of duty that will then confront me. I shall ask the Congress for the one remaining instrument to meet the crisis—broad executive power to wage war against the emergency."

Roosevelt's first one hundred days in office revealed the extent of executive power he sought and the willingness of Congress to grant him that power. Soon after taking office, Roosevelt called Congress into special session. He asked the House of Representatives and the Senate to accept a series of measures designed to relieve the economic hardships the nation was experiencing, and he asked that these measures be accepted speedily without undue deliberation and debate.

To facilitate the passage of the President's legislation through the House, the House Rules Committee placed ten of Roosevelt's bills under what were known as "closed rules." The rules were first drafted by the committee and then quickly passed by a majority vote. The closed rules made it impossible to introduce new amendments to a bill after it left committee, waived points of order, and severely limited debate. Under these rules, the Emergency Banking Bill passed the House in thirty-eight minutes. Later the same day, it was passed by the Senate after only two hours and fifteen minutes of deliberation.

Early the next year, 1934, the House Rules Committee issued a ruling that forbade for the rest of that session of Congress all amendments to appropriations bills that would conflict with the economic program accepted the previous year. This step was taken to prevent Roosevelt's opponents from watering down the President's legislation. Protests were lodged by the Republicans, who called it "the most vicious, the most far-reaching special rule" ever issued by the House Rules Committee. But the protesters were unable to halt the President's power over Congress at this time. Many new bills were passed, including the Emergency Relief

Act, the National Industrial Recovery Act, the Tennessee Valley Authority Act, and the Economy Act.

Roosevelt's special relationship with Congress lasted through his first term in office. Democratic leaders in the House of Representatives and the Senate regarded it as their clear duty to support the President's programs in every way possible. During his second term, however, this relationship began to disintegrate. Conservative, mostly southern representatives began to gain control of the House and to use their power to block the President's programs. Anti-Roosevelt feeling centered in the Rules Committee, which fought the President tooth and nail and which used its power on several occasions to undermine his prestige and authority.

The Senate was likewise characterized by a growing distrust of the President. When Roosevelt attempted to gain Senate support to pack the Supreme Court with men who favored the President's policies after the court had declared several of his New Deal programs unconstitutional, the Senate rebelled. Senators protested that the President had intruded too far into the affairs of the Senate and had undermined its independence. When Roosevelt responded by campaigning against several senators he disliked in an effort to get them defeated in the fall elections of 1938 (an effort that failed), the relationship between the President and the Senate chilled to a new low.

A second expansion of presidential authority under Roosevelt came after the Japanese invasion of Pearl Harbor on December 7, 1941, and America's entry into World War II. The President immediately assumed broad wartime emergency powers on the basis of his constitutional title of commander in chief of the armed forces. "The President has powers," he declared, "under the Constitution and under Congressional acts to take measures necessary to avert a disaster." Roosevelt added that these powers would "revert to the people" once the war was over, but that now he needed to exercise them.

Roosevelt did not hesitate to use his wartime powers to exert his authority over Congress. On one occasion, he warned the Congress that he would fail to carry out a bill it was about to pass, and Congress tabled the legislation rather than confront the President. Vast new agencies were likewise created by the chief executive to manage the nation's participation in the war. In most cases, these agencies were established without the specific consent of Congress. The House and Senate tacitly agreed to their existence—the wartime agencies were, after all, necessary and essential—but did not provide a legal basis for them by the passage of new legislation. This failure can be excused because of the emergency created by the war, but it nevertheless helped to establish a dangerous precedent. In the name of national security, future Presidents could feel justified in using their authority to establish new agencies without the consent of Congress.

Roosevelt was a popular President who was elected to four terms in office. Although that popularity had begun to wane by his fourth term, he still had the support of large numbers of people who respected his leadership ability and who had little sympathy with the opposition the President had encountered in Congress. Roosevelt had called the Senate "a bunch of incompetent obstructionists" and had said that the American people "want their government to act, and not merely to talk." Most of the nation agreed with him. *Action* was the basis of his program whether in dealing with the domestic problems caused by the Great Depression or in handling the wartime needs and concerns of the nation. By comparison with the President, Congress seemed to be cursed by inaction and immobility. Roosevelt's strong leadership established the tradition of the imperial president; after him the nation would look to the chief executive for solutions to the country's problems and expect little from Congress except compliance with the President's will.

II

Harry Truman, who became President upon the death of Roosevelt in 1945, inherited a pugnacious and unmanageable Congress. The House and Senate still resented the late President's use of power and looked at his successor with suspicion. Truman had served in the Senate where he had chaired a committee that looked into wartime expenditures. He was known to be a loyal Democrat who had worked his way up through the party machine in Missouri. Many in Washington regarded him as a lightweight with little experience or ability to bring to the presidency. Yet Truman, like Roosevelt, expanded the powers of his office and must be regarded as one of the imperial Presidents.

The pugnacious Congress Truman inherited refused to consider most of his program for domestic legislation, which he called the Fair Deal.* But it did follow his leadership in matters of war and foreign affairs. The crises presented by the Great Depression and World War II had come to an end only to be replaced by a new emergency in some ways graver than the earlier ones. The Soviet Union expanded its power in Eastern Europe; China, after decades of revolution, became a communist nation. Even though the United States did not face imminent invasion, these moves were regarded with fear by most Americans. Was the whole world soon to fall victim to communist revolution? Should America stand

* This rebellious Congress was also responsible for the Twenty-Second Amendment to the Constitution, which limited the number of terms a President could serve to two. The amendment was a slap at Roosevelt, who had been elected to four terms.

idly by while nation after nation fell under the power of Moscow?

What emerged during this crisis was a "bipartisan foreign policy." Republican leaders and others in the House and Senate might object to the President's domestic policies, but they would stand by him in the cold war against the Soviet Union and give him their support in the name of national unity and solidarity. With the help of Congress, Truman developed the Marshall Plan for the reconstruction of war-torn Europe and other measures designed "to stem the communist advance." The bipartisan foreign policy was an important asset to the President in a time of crisis and an act that placed patriotism above party spirit. But at the same time, it was detrimental to the development of the House and Senate and a blow to legislative government, because it undermined the ability of Congress to debate the policies of the President and effectively to criticize them.

One of the most important issues during the Truman presidency was the Korean War. On June 24, 1950, the army of communist North Korea invaded South Korea, a nation friendly to the United States. A resolution passed by the United Nations condemned the invasion, and Truman, using his emergency powers, decided to commit American air and sea forces to aid South Korea as part of a concerted effort by members of the UN. Later, the American army was committed as well. Two days after his decision, Truman met with a bipartisan delegation from Congress and received its support for his actions.

But Truman decided not to ask for legislation from the whole Congress in favor of the war. Instead, his advisers cited many precedents for Presidents sending troops into combat on their own initiative without consultation with Congress. In the Senate, Paul Douglas (Democrat, Illinois) defended the President's actions by arguing that modern warfare made immediate action necessary, the sort of action Congress could not exert. "With tanks, airplanes, and the atom bomb," he said, "war can become instantaneous and disaster can occur while Congress is assembling and debating."

But conservative members of Congress disagreed. Senator Robert Taft, who supported the President's use of force against North Korea, nevertheless added that Truman had "no legal authority" to do what he had done. Representative Frederic Coudert, Jr. (Republican, New York), chastized the House and Senate for their inability to challenge the President when he exceeded his authority. "How devastating a precedent they have set," Coudert said, "in remaining silent while the President took over the powers specifically reserved for Congress in the Constitution." Edwin Corwin, a scholar and student of government, put it another way. It was a paradox, he wrote, that Congress had been reduced to a mere rubber stamp for the President's policies in the name of preserving free institutions.

In April, 1952, when workers in the steel industry threatened to strike, Truman once again made use of his wartime authority and directed the Department of Commerce to nationalize the steel mills. He declared that his action, which he took reluctantly, was in the name of national security because a steel strike would lead to a cutoff of valuable war materials for Korea.

Nationalization was an unprecedented step in American history. In this case, Truman was careful to consult with Congress and to ask its advice on his move, but the Congress failed to respond. "I have twice sent messages to the Congress asking it to prescribe a course [of action]," Truman said. "If the Congress disagreed with the action I was taking," he said, it had not said so. The steel companies took the case to the Supreme Court, which decided against nationalization, six to three. In the end, it had been the courts, not Congress, that had limited the power of the President.

But Truman stood by his conception of the presidency. "The President of the United States," he declared, "has very great powers to meet great national emergencies." When asked if this meant that a President could seize newspapers or radio stations in a time of crisis, Truman responded, "the President of the United States has to act for whatever is for the best of the country. That's the answer."

III

DWIGHT EISENHOWER came to the presidency in 1953 with no experience in government. He had been a hero of World War II, a great general who had been supreme commander of the Allied forces in Europe. Eisenhower was elected as a Republican and shared the view of many Republicans and conservatives that Presidents Roosevelt and Truman had usurped too much power and that it was time to limit the authority of the President. Yet Eisenhower too came to broaden the power of the presidency in new and important ways.

The Eisenhower administration, for instance, was responsible for the notion of "executive privilege." On May 17, 1954, Eisenhower sent a letter to his secretary of defense that claimed it an absolute right of the President to withhold information from Congress. He claimed this right in the name of national security. "It is essential to efficient and effective administration," Eisenhower wrote, "that employees of the executive branch be in a position to be completely candid in advising with each other on official matters." This could not be done, the President implied, if the Congress was permitted wholesale access to executive department material.

The doctrine of executive privilege meant that the President and the whole executive branch could operate in complete secrecy, with no interference from congressional investigatory committees or from individual members of Congress. Eisenhower said that it was not in the public interest that any executive conversations or communications, any documents or reproductions be made available to Congress. The list of such material was a long one and included "interdepartmental memoranda, advisory opinions, recommendations of subordinates, informal working papers, material in personnel files, and the like."

Earlier Presidents had claimed that conversations and communications with their aides and cabinet members were privileged, and the Congress had generally accepted this practice. What Eisenhower had done, however, was to expand the notion of privilege to cover the whole executive branch. The cold war climate in Washington led many to accept the President's right to withhold information, but others found fault with it. Clark Mollenhoff, for instance, pointed out that earlier scandals involving the President and his advisers, such as the Teapot Dome Scandal during the Harding administration, "could have been covered up if government officials had then applied even the mildest form of executive privilege as laid down by President Eisenhower." At the same time, Telford Taylor claimed that executive privilege, in practice, would shut the House and Senate off "from access to documents to which they are clearly entitled by tradition, common sense, and good governmental practice." The Eisenhower administration, however, defended executive privilege and exercised it several times during the next few years.

With the help of Congress, Eisenhower also expanded the President's war-making authority. He consulted with the House and Senate to gain support for a program of military aid he planned for Formosa and the Middle East. Congress responded with a blanket resolution giving the President broad powers to act as he saw fit. The resolution named no specific enemy, except as the President might decide. Indeed, congressional opposition to granting Eisenhower this enormous responsibility was almost nonexistent. House Speaker Sam Rayburn spoke for the majority in Congress when he said, "We are not going to take the responsibility out of the hands of the constitutional leader and try to arrogate it to ourselves." And, Rayburn added, if the President had acted on his own without the formality of consulting Congress, "he would have had no criticism from me."

There was at least one critic of expanded presidential authority in Congress, however, and that was Senator William Fulbright (Democrat, Arkansas), who was a member of the Senate Foreign Relations Committee. Fulbright wondered why Congress should "abdicate its constitutional powers" so easily. He regretted that the "suspense and urgency" of the cold war led the President to actions that seemed "designed to manage Congress, to coerce it into signing this blank check" for presidential authority. If the House and Senate continued to submit so readily to the President's requests, Fulbright warned, the time would come when future Presidents would cease to consult with Congress at all.

IV

THE ADMINISTRATION of John Kennedy was too short for history to judge what his attitude toward the expansion of presidential authority was. Many historians agree that his most dramatic use of emergency power, during the Cuban missile crisis of 1962, was warranted by the severity of the threat to the security of the United States. Others, however, point out that President Kennedy did nothing during his three-year presidency to diffuse the powers he had inherited from Franklin Roosevelt, Truman, and Eisenhower.

It was under Lyndon Johnson, who became President after Kennedy's assassination in November, 1963, that presidential authority once again began to expand. Johnson was a man who enjoyed the exercise of power. He had served in the House of Representatives and later in the Senate, where he had been one of the most effective majority leaders of all time. As a member of Congress, Johnson had greatly admired President Roosevelt and had supported Truman's and Eisenhower's use of emergency powers durin the cold war.

In his book, *The Twilight of the Presidency*, George Reedy has left us a striking description of Johnson in the White House. Reedy served as Johnson's press secretary and knew the President intimately. Members of Congress, Reedy wrote, showed Johnson a respect similar to the respect shown by a vassal to his lord when brought into the presidential presence: "The wise senator enters cautiously, dressed in his Sunday best and with a respectful, almost pious look on his face." If the senator dares to disagree with the President on some issue, Reedy continued, he shows this disagreement in a "most deferential, almost apologetic" manner. The aura of majesty around the President, he concluded, was "so universal that the slightest hint of criticism automatically labels a man as a colossal lout."

Very early in his administration, Johnson revealed that he would be a strong chief executive who would not hesitate to use the full powers of his office. He worked closely with Congress—whose practices and procedures he understood thoroughly—to develop a program of social and economic reform similar to the New Deal legislation of Franklin Roosevelt's first term as President. Like Roosevelt, Johnson was a man who prized action and achievement above talk and deliberation.

It was in the areas of war and foreign affairs, however, that Johnson exercised powers that critics believed belonged to the House of Representatives and the Senate. In the spring of 1965, Johnson sent 22,000 American troops into the Dominican Republic without the approval of Congress. His reason, he stated, was to save American lives, which he thought to be endangered. But the 22,000 troops were far more than were necessary to rescue the Americans in that country. The maneuver was actually a show of force designed to put down a possible communist takeover, a takeover that many observers familiar with affairs in the Dominican Republic claimed was not about to happen. What Johnson had done, critics pointed out, was to use presidential authority to settle a political problem in another country. The problem posed no immediate threat to the United States, nor was America in danger of being invaded. Did the invasion of the Dominican Republic, they asked, mean that a President could act alone to involve America in any problem that arose in another country? If so, what had happened to the clear wording of the Constitution that told the President to work with Congress in such matters?

But Johnson's great usurpation of power came over the question of the Vietnam War. For many years—since long before Johnson came to office—South Vietnam had been engulfed in revolution and civil war. The issue was ticklish because the rebels in South Vietnam had the open support of communist North Vietnam. Presidents Eisenhower and Kennedy had sent military aid and advisers to South Vietnam, but had looked upon the war as one that would have to be won or lost by the South Vietnamese themselves. Johnson, on the other hand, in keeping with the cold war belief that communism must be confronted wherever it arises, came to believe that the Vietnam War would have to be "Americanized," that is, fought with the strong assistance of the American military.

Johnson ordered American troops by the thousands into South Vietnam and told the air force to begin the bombing of North Vietnam. He took this action on the basis of the Tonkin Gulf Resolution, which had been passed by Congress in August, 1964. Experts would later disagree on whether the President had deliberately deceived Congress into passing the resolution or whether Congress had been the victim of misinformation and hasty action. In any case, the resolution strongly supported the President and said that Congress "approves and supports the determination of the President, as Commander in Chief, to take all necessary measures to repel any armed attack against the forces of the United States and to prevent further aggression." The resolution passed the House without any opposition and received only two dissenting votes in the Senate.

As the Vietnam War grew unpopular throughout the country, the resolution was questioned from two directions. Conservatives like Senator Sam Ervin, regarded as an authority on the Constitution, believed that in passing the resolution Congress had delegated its war-making authority entirely to the President. This had established a dangerous precedent, he argued, because it upset the constitutional balance of power between the executive and the legislature and left the Congress no means by which it could check the actions of the President.

Others, ignoring the constitutional issue, claimed that Johnson had manufactured the Tonkin Gulf crisis to trick Congress into passing the resolution. They blamed the war on the President and implied that Congress would never have supported him if it had known the truth. The conservatives were closer to the truth. The Tonkin Gulf Resolution was simply another example of the willingness of Congress to turn its powers over to the President and avoid its constitutional responsibility to assist the President in matters facing the nation. Two senators questioned the resolution and called for more debate, but the vast majority in the House and Senate allowed their authority to slide into the hands of the President. It was a decision many would later regret and one that would be withdrawn during the years of congressional change and reform that characterized the seventies.

V

THE IMPERIAL presidency reached its highest point during the administration of Richard Nixon. Other Presidents had expanded the war-making powers of the presidency, defended "executive privilege," and emphasized the importance of presidential supremacy in matters of foreign affairs. But they had continued to allow Congress to play a part in domestic issues. Even Franklin Roosevelt and Lyndon Johnson worked through the House and Senate to achieve their important legislative programs. Although they seemed at times to dominate Congress by the force of their wills and by their enormous political skills, they did not subvert the constitutional role Congress must play in domestic affairs.

Nixon, however, had much grander notions of presidential authority. A skilled, intelligent politician, he had served in the House of Representatives and the Senate, rising rapidly in Republican party circles to become Vice-President under Dwight Eisenhower. When he was elected President in 1968, it was on a platform that promised less governmental control of American life, less government spending, and reform of the bureaucracy.

But Nixon was attracted by the trappings of power. As President, he made several changes in White House customs that revealed his conception of the presidency. He dressed White House security guards in uniforms that resembled the livery worn by the attendants of European monarchs of old and that made the guards look to many like characters from nineteenth century comic operas such as "The Merry Widow." He instituted the use of ceremonial trumpets in state affairs at the executive mansion. He used federal money to make improvements on his two private estates—one in Florida and one in California—improvements that included carpeting, trees, swimming-pool heaters, and golf carts, among other things. But these were only the outward signs of a deeper need for power and authority.

During his first term in office, Nixon centralized authority around himself, even to the exclusion of his cabinet. He had forty-eight personal assistants, compared with twenty-three for Kennedy and twenty for Johnson. In 1971, the White House payroll listed

600 employees, well over twice the number (266) that had worked there during the Eisenhower years. The executive office staff, during the same period, had grown from 1,175 to 5,395.* This large body of assistants and staff members—many of whom made important decisions and possessed a great deal of power—were not subject to congressional approval, like other presidential appointments to high office. They were the President's own men and women, loyal to his policies and decisions, and willing to put them into effect.

Other Presidents, of course, have had staff and aides who have been loyal and hardworking. But what set Nixon's White House apart from previous ones was the size of the staff and the purposes for which it was used: Nixon's large number of assistants was to be used as part of the President's program to bring order to the federal government and to the nation. If Congress was irresponsible and spendthrift, the President would find a way to control spending on his own. If critics of the President were too vocal, a means to silence them could be found. In short, Nixon's large staff was essential if he was to function as the strong President he wanted to be.

Nixon inherited Lyndon Johnson's war in Vietnam and promised to bring it to an honorable end. In the spring of 1970, as part of his program to end the war as quickly as possible, he ordered the invasion of Cambodia, a country neighboring Vietnam that had remained officially neutral during the war. Nixon ordered the invasion secretly and later defended it as an effort necessary to save American lives. Enemy soldiers used Cambodia as a haven from which to attack American troops and installations in Vietnam, he declared, and this enemy haven had to be brought under control.

* Compare these figures with Herbert Hoover's staff. Hoover had *two* personal secretaries when he came to office, but he was able to persuade Congress to grant him a third.

William Rehnquist, then an assistant attorney general and now an associate justice of the Supreme Court, was chosen by the President to write a legal defense of the invasion. Rehnquist's defense relied primarily on the President's role as commander in chief, but also cited precedents established by earlier Presidents acting in similar circumstances. If the Commander in Chief of the Armed Forces, Rehnquist argued, discovered that a neutral country housed enemy forces that were potentially dangerous to the United States, didn't he have the right to order an invasion of that country?

Nixon's many critics, however, believed otherwise. If the President, they asked, had the authority secretly to decide to invade a neutral country, where did that authority stop? Could he expand the war on his own to include Laos and China? Even Lyndon Johnson, they pointed out, who had begun the enormous American commitment in Vietnam, had rejected recommendations from military experts who wanted to expand the war into neutral areas.

But the strongest argument against the invasion and Nixon's use of power came from a precedent set by Abraham Lincoln. Lincoln, President during the Civil War, had to quiet public fears that British troops would invade the United States from Canada in support of the Confederacy. When told he had the power to authorize a preventive invasion of Canada, Lincoln replied, "Allow the President to invade a neighboring nation, whenever he shall deem it necessary to repel invasion . . . and you allow him to make war at pleasure. Study and see if you can fix any limit to his power in this respect." The Constitution, Lincoln added, provided that no one man shall be able to bring the country into war, but that war should be the responsibility of Congress as well as the President.

The year after the Cambodian invasion, in 1971, Nixon continued to avoid consultation with Congress on problems involved with the war. The House and Senate, where antiwar sentiment was now strong, approved an amendment to the Defense Procurement Authorization Act of that year, which said it was "the policy of the United States to terminate at the earliest practicable date all military operations of the United States in Indochina." The amendment had no bite, however, because Congress had made no effort to cut off funds for the war—the one move it could have made to underline its seriousness about ending the war. When he signed the act into law, Nixon simply declared that the amendment did not "represent the policies of the administration. My signing of the bill that contains this section . . . will not change the policies I have pursued." Senator Frank Church (Democrat, Idaho) found Nixon's attitude contemptuous. "A century ago," he said, "it is inconceivable that a chief executive would have disregarded a statute, let alone dismiss its provisions in such an abrupt and peremptory way. That Mr. Nixon felt no compunction in doing so is a reflection of the low estate to which the Congress has fallen."

The "low estate" of Congress was also reflected in Nixon's efforts to expand the powers of the President in domestic affairs. During his six years in office, Nixon attempted to establish greater presidential control of spending. He tried to impose restraints on the freedom of the press and to expand the investigative powers of the FBI and CIA. At every step, according to historian Arthur Schlesinger, Jr., Nixon's moves were guided by a desire to acquire more power over the federal government and to bypass Congress. He wanted, Schlesinger adds, to govern by presidential decree rather than have his programs and policies watered down or destroyed by the House and Senate.

At one point, for instance, Nixon tried to phase out an agency—the Office of Economic Opportunity (OEO)—that Congress had voted to allow to continue. On another occasion, he added powers by executive fiat to an agency that many in Congress had long regarded as useless, the Subversive Activities Control Board. In the first case, Nixon was stopped by the courts, which declared the administration's tactics illegal. In the second, he was stopped by an irate Senate that voted to forbid the use of appropriated funds to carry out the executive order.

In the matter of government spending, Nixon expanded presidential power by use of "impoundment." Through impoundment, the President could refuse to spend money that had already been appropriated by Congress. William Rehnquist, who had supported the invasion of Cambodia, warned Nixon that impoundment, as he proposed to practice it, was neither reasonable nor constitutional, but the President went ahead with his plans anyway. Money was impounded in the areas of clean air and water programs, health, defense, housing, and education appropriations.

The problem with Nixon's use of impoundment was that it was done to curtail or terminate legislation already passed by Congress without the use of the presidential veto. Impoundment ignored the traditional responsibility of the House of Representatives to set appropriations and of the Senate to concur in these appropriations. If followed to its logical conclusion, impoundment could mean complete presidential control of government spending—a clear violation of the Constitution. Once again, it was Senator Sam Ervin who underlined the constitutional difficulties of impoundment. Impoundment, he said, had become "a means whereby the White House can give effect to social goals of its own choosing by reallocating national resources in contravention of congressional dictates." Impoundment, he concluded, enabled the President "to modify, reshape, or nullify completely laws passed by the legislative branch, thereby making legislative policy—a power reserved exclusively to the Congress."

Other Nixon targets were the press and other communications media. For almost as long as he had been in public office, Nixon had regarded the media with suspicion and had maintained that they depicted him unfairly. As President, he moved along several fronts to challenge newspapers and television and to force them to accept his view of what the media should be. Nixon's Vice-President, Spiro Agnew, the acting head of the FBI, and other high government officials were enlisted in the campaign and went about the country attacking the press for its negativism and disparagement of the President. The media were accused of being too "liberal" to represent the opinions of average Americans and reporters were denounced for their lack of patriotism and love for American institutions.

When confronted by the case of the Pentagon papers—a set of secret documents relating to the Vietnam War—the President attempted to impose prior restraint on their publication by the *Washington Post* and the *New York Times*—the first time in American history that the government had attempted prior restraint on the press. On another occasion, the head of the White House Office of Telecommunications warned that the federal government might refuse to renew the licenses of television and radio stations that failed "to correct imbalance or consistent bias" in their news programs. The government, of course, would decide what constituted imbalance and bias. And on yet another occasion, a White House aide said that the administration would subject the major networks to antitrust suits if they did not "move conservatives and people with a viewpoint of Middle America onto the networks." What had happened, said Senator Sam Ervin, was that the administration had "assaulted the very integrity of the press and called into question its right to disagree with official views."

But there was an even more sinister side to Nixon's exercise of authority. This was his need to know what went on among his opponents—whom he regarded as his "enemies"—and to control rebellious elements in American society. Nixon came to office at a time of great national ferment. Two national leaders, Robert Kennedy and Martin Luther King, Jr., had recently been assassinated. Uprisings among discontented blacks had scarred major American cities, and the antiwar movement had grown large and vocal. Left wing political groups were stronger than they had been in any period since the 1930s.

Nixon feared that this social and political discontent could be traced to foreign subversion. He likewise came to believe that the American intelligence community—the FBI, the CIA, the National Security Agency, and the Defense Intelligence Agency—would have to be strengthened if order and harmony were to be restored to the nation. With this in mind, he called the heads of these agencies to the White House to discuss plans for the future.

The result was a decision memorandum issued by the President in July, 1970. The memorandum gave presidential authorization to the agencies for breaking and entering (or "burglary," as one Nixon aide called it) for purposes of gaining information. It recommended that undercover agents be planted in universities, the source of much of the unrest, and that the CIA investigate students and other Americans living abroad. The memorandum also advocated the electronic surveillance of Americans "who pose a major threat to the internal security" of the United States, and it gave power to the agencies to listen to international phone calls and to open and copy mail.

The program failed to materialize, largely because of the opposition of J. Edgar Hoover, head of the FBI. But the state of mind behind the program continued to exist. Because the intelligence agencies had failed to follow his program, Nixon created his own group to investigate his opponents and "enemies." Run by members of Nixon's White House staff, the office was given the name "the Plumbers," because it was intended to stop leaks of information. One of its first tasks, under orders from the President, was to find out everything it could about Daniel Ellsberg, the man responsible for the leakage of the Pentagon papers. The Plumbers responded by burglarizing the offices of Ellsberg's psychiatrist in hope of finding the information they sought.

The state of mind that created the Plumbers likewise led to Watergate. In the summer of 1972, during the presidential campaign that would lead to Nixon's second term in office, six men were discovered late at night in the headquarters of the Democratic National Committee in Washington, D. C. Later investigation showed they had been sent there by men close to Nixon in order to find information about the Democratic campaign. The "Watergate affair" dominated Washington political life for more than a year and caused President Nixon to invoke executive privilege as a means to prevent investigation of his activities. What the men who were sent to the Watergate "were trying to steal," Sam Ervin said, "was not the jewels, money, or other property of American citizens, but something more valuable—the most precious heritage, the right to vote in a free election."

Journalist Walter Lippmann put it another way. "Watergate," he wrote, "shows how very vulnerable our constitutional system is. If the national government falls into the hands of sufficiently unprincipled and unscrupulous men, they can do terrible things before anyone can stop them." Watergate was the result of an attempt by the President and his people to accumulate too much power into the hands of the President. Lincoln had said that "no one man" should have the power to bring the nation into war. He could have added that "no one man" was meant to control the federal government.

But if Nixon can be seen as a villain who abused his powers as President, he can also be regarded as an unwitting hero. By pressing the powers of the President to the extreme, Nixon aroused the fears of Congress as they have rarely been aroused. By circumventing Congress in so many areas—through the invasion of Cambodia, the impoundment of funds, and his domestic excesses—

Nixon had made the Congress, and the American public, realize that the Constitution, as it had been framed by the Founding Fathers, had been distorted and ignored by the imperial Presidents. It was now time to redress the balance. Throughout the period of the imperial Presidents, Congress had made attempts to reassert its powers and authority. The crises of the Vietnam War and the Nixon years gave it the impetus it needed to complete the task.

CHAPTER SIX

PRELIMINARY STEPS TOWARD REFORM

Congress must modernize its machinery and methods if it is to keep pace with a greatly enlarged and active executive branch. This is a better approach than that which seeks to meet the problem by reducing and hamstringing the executive. A strong and more representative legislature, in touch with and better informed about the administration, is the antidote to bureaucracy—FROM A 1945 REPORT OF THE AMERICAN POLITICAL SCIENCE ASSOCIATION

BY 1945, the last year of World War II, Congress was under a great deal of pressure to reform. This pressure came from professional organizations, in forms such as the quotation from the American Political Science Association cited above, from newspaper editors, and other private sources. But it likewise came from Congress itself. "In the midst of this war," said Jerry Voorhis (Democrat, California) on January 18, 1945, in a speech before the House of Representatives, "we have to grant executive power . . . of the most sweeping nature" to the President. But once this war has come to an end, he declared, this practice must come to an end. New congressional habits must be established "in order that this Congress may perform its functions efficiently, effectively, and in accord with the needs of the people of this nation." Congress must not be, he went on, "merely an agency that says yes or no to executive proposals, but an agency capable of, and actually performing the function of bringing forth its own constructive program for the needs of the people of this nation. Thus it will take its place and keep its place as an altogether coequal branch of our government."

The problems with Congress that cried out for change were obvious to many. Committees dominated both houses, and power was concentrated in the hands of a few influential—and often dictatorial—committee chairmen. Complex rules and procedures slowed down the work of the House of Representatives and were exploited by conservative minorities often at odds with the majority, while filibusters stalled Senate activity. The practice of seniority prevented younger and often talented representatives and senators from exercising responsibility in congressional affairs. Among the public, the power and prestige of the presidency was on the rise, whereas that of Congress was in sharp decline. As the report from the American Political Science Association and Representative Voorhis's statements implied, the machinery of Congress—its ability to respond to problems in an immediate and meaningful way—had worn down and was in need of repair.

I

THE PRESSURE for change led the House and Senate to create the Joint Committee on the Organization of Congress in February, 1945. Six members from each house, evenly divided between Democrats and Republicans, were chosen to sit on the committee. The committee chairman was Senator Robert La Follette, Jr.

(Progressive, Wisconsin), and its vice-chairman was Representative Mike Monroney (Democrat, Oklahoma), both of whom were strong advocates of reform.

Over the next four months, the joint committee heard testimony from members of Congress and experts in governmental affairs. Much of the testimony centered on complaints about the committee system, but other issues were raised, such as changes in the Rules Committee, the method of drawing up the legislative budget, and the relationship between Congress and the President. After several additional months of consideration, a final report was submitted to Congress and became the basis for the Legislative Reorganization Act of 1946.

The reform act attacked the committee problem from several angles. First, the number of standing committees in the House of Representatives was reduced from forty-eight to nineteen and that of the Senate from thirty-three to fifteen. Obsolete committees or committees with little work to perform were eliminated. In addition, all standing committees, with the exception of the Appropriations Committee, were directed to establish regular meeting days, to keep complete records of committee activities, including the way members voted on bills, and to open all hearings to the public except hearings held in special executive sessions. In the House, committee chairmen were expected to report any bill to the floor for vote if a majority of committee members favored the bill.

These measures helped to simplify and streamline committee structure and to lighten the congressional workload. But more important, they also served to lessen the absolute power of committee chairmen, if ever so lightly. Committee meetings now could not be called at the whim of the chairman, nor could committee activities be kept secret. Moreover, with the publication of a journal of committee activities, committee members would have to show greater responsibility than in the past for the positions they took during committee meetings. Gone were the days when a representative could work against a bill in closed session and then support the bill on the House floor, where his actions could be known to his constituents back home.

Another important provision of the Legislative Reorganization Act of 1946 * granted each standing committee the right to hire four professional and six clerical staff members. The professional staff helped senators and representatives to master the complex and sometimes highly technical material that cropped up from time to time during committee activities. The clerical staff took care of the growing amount of paperwork every congressional committee has faced in the twentieth century. The act also made the Legislative Reference Service a separate division of the Library of Congress, so that it could better handle requests from members of Congress for information and research on issues before the House and Senate.

Most senators and representatives regarded the Legislative Reorganization Act as a significant step toward modernizing and improving the functioning and structure of Congress. But as time passed, its failures and shortcomings became obvious. The act had not dealt with seniority, nor had it addressed the problems of the relationship between Congress and the President. The reduction of the number of House and Senate committees had gotten rid of a lot of deadwood, but it had strengthened the power and autonomy of the remaining committees, giving them and their chairmen even greater importance than they earlier had had. These problems and others would have to be solved by later Congresses.

* Section Three of the act required that all lobbyists register with the clerk of the House. It was the first step Congress had taken against lobbying, but because it made no attempt to control the methods lobbyists used, it lacked real bite.

II

One of the frequent complaints made by witnesses before the Joint Committee on the Organization of Congress concerned the House Rules Committee. Since 1937, the committee had been dominated by a group of conservative Democrats and Republicans who used their power—the Rules Committee decides how legislation will be considered on the House floor—to block bills they considered too liberal. Some witnesses maintained that the Rules Committee's power should be limited to deciding the order in which bills would be considered on the floor and should not include the power to kill a bill. Others wanted bills to be brought before the House by a unanimous vote from the committee that drew up the bill, without reference to the Rules Committee. In any case, the joint committee did not reach a decision on the Rules Committee, because it could reach no agreement on how it should be reformed.

In 1948, however, the Rules Committee once again proved to be obstructive. It refused to release a housing bill sponsored by the Banking and Currency Committee until provisions for public housing and slum clearance were deleted. When a newly elected and more liberal House of Representatives took office in January of the next year, hope swelled that some changes could be made.

Led by Speaker Sam Rayburn, the Democratic caucus voted 176 to 48 to accept what was known as the "21-day rule." This rule gave the chairman of any committee the right to bring a bill to the House floor, if he had requested a rule from the Rules Committee and the Rules Committee had failed to act within twenty-one calendar days of his request.* The House quickly ac-

* The 21-day rule pertained to bills that had been approved by a majority of their sponsoring committee. Committee chairmen on their own could not release bills to get a ruling from the Rules Committee.

cepted the new rule and during that session of Congress, it was used eight times to release bills blocked by the Rules Committee. Two years later, however, it was voted down by a House dominated by Republicans and conservatives. Representative Charles Halleck (Republican, Indiana) said that he opposed the 21-day rule because it prevented the Rules Committee from putting a stop to all "unwise, unsound, ill-timed, spendthrift, and socialistic measures" that came before the House.

For the next few years, the Rules Committee continued to function as it had before. After 1955, its chairman was Howard W. Smith (Democrat, Virginia), whose power became legendary. An old-fashioned southerner, Smith stood firmly against all civil rights bills and all legislation that he believed would strengthen the federal government at the expense of the states. He could delay or destroy legislation that his committee had to consider merely by retiring to his Virginia estate, because the committee could not meet for business without the presence of the chairman.

The next important attempt at change came during the administration of President John Kennedy, who took office in 1961. Kennedy was a Democrat who favored a broad legislative program of social and economic reform—exactly the sort of legislation that Smith and most of the members of the Rules Committee opposed. Fearful that Kennedy's program would be destroyed by the Rules Committee, House liberals and the new President began to look for ways to overcome the committee's power. Speaker Rayburn, who had a personal distaste for change and preferred to work with the House as he knew it, reluctantly agreed to join their cause.

Rayburn's plan was to increase the size of the committee from twelve to fifteen, with the addition of two new Democrats and one Republican. The two Democrats would be chosen because of their loyalty to the President and could be used to create a majority on the committee in favor of the administration's policies. The plan was strongly opposed by Chairman Smith and Minority Leader Halleck and other conservative Democrats and Republicans. But after a month of hard work and back-room maneuvering, Rayburn saw it through the House by the close vote of 217 to 212.

The enlargement of the Rules Committee, however, brought the liberals only limited success. Conservatives from time to time were still able to muster enough votes to kill bills they did not like, particularly bills connected with civil rights and the affairs of black Americans. By 1965, a renewed call for change on the part of the liberals resulted in the readoption of the 21-day rule as well as two other rules that helped to limit the power of the committee. But two years later a more conservative-minded House voted once again to dispense with the 21-day rule.

What finally served to bring an end to the old southern- and conservative-dominated committee was not a change in rules, but the defeat of its chairman. In 1966, the eighty-three-year-old Smith lost in a primary election to another Democrat. The chairmanship of the Rules Committee by seniority then moved to another conservative southerner, William Colmer (Democrat, Mississippi). But Colmer did not possess the political skills the former chairman had possessed, nor did he have the ability to dominate an influential committee. Liberal Democrats attempted to have Colmer removed from the chairmanship, but when this failed, they were able to demand several significant changes in Rules Committee procedures.

For the first time, the committee was required to have written rules so that its activities would not be subject to the whims of its chairman. These written rules included requirements for regularly scheduled weekly meetings and allowed the ranking majority member on the committee to call and preside at meetings in the absence of the chairman. The new rules also required the consent of a majority to table a bill and set limits on proxy voting * by members. With these reforms, which were adopted in 1967, more than two decades of demands for changes in the Rules Committee came to an end.

III

WHILE LIBERALS in the House of Representatives struggled against the Rules Committee, liberals and others in the Senate looked for a way to limit the filibuster. Cloture—the attempt to stop filibustering by a two-thirds vote—had proved inadequate in most cases, and although cloture was called for on eight different occasions between 1938 and 1946, it was defeated in each instance. The chief target of filibustering had now become civil rights legislation. Bills that would have destroyed the poll tax—a tactic used in the southern states to prevent blacks from voting—were successfully filibustered in 1942, 1944, and 1946, and a bill for fair employment practices for blacks was filibustered in 1946.

What made the cloture rule so difficult to invoke was a series of rulings and precedents that made it impossible to apply cloture to debates on procedural questions. This made it possible for filibusterers to tie up Senate business long before a final vote was reached on a controversial bill. Indeed, those rulings and precedents had become so complex by 1948 that Arthur Vandenberg (Republican, Michigan), the president pro tempore, concluded that "in the final analysis, the Senate has no effective cloture rule at all."

The next year, a liberal attempt to strengthen the cloture rule

* Proxy voting was a system practiced both on the House floor and in the committees. A representative who knew he was to be absent from a vote would give his vote to another representative to cast.

backfired. Conservative Democrats and Republicans joined forces to oppose any change, which they feared would give the Truman administration the opportunity to pass civil rights legislation it supported. So great was the opposition to change that the conservative coalition was able to push through a new cloture rule, one that was more restrictive than the earlier rule had been. Under the new rule, two-thirds of the whole Senate was needed to invoke cloture, rather than two-thirds of those present and voting. Furthermore, the new rule prevented cloture from applying to debate on motions to change the Senate rules, to which it had previously applied. This made it virtually impossible to change Senate rules, since filibusterers could tie up any discussion of change and reform.

Closed off from any effective means to limit the filibuster, Senate liberals began to look for another way to tackle the problem. Attempts to get the Senate to adopt its rules at the beginning of each new Congress and thereby bring the cloture rule up for consideration on a regular basis ended in failure in 1953 and 1957. In 1957, liberals were supported by Vice-President Richard Nixon, who offered an "advisory opinion" in his role as president of the Senate. Nixon pointed out that the Constitution provides that "each house may determine the rules of its proceedings." What this meant, the Vice-President said, was that the Senate could adopt new rules "under whatever procedures the majority of the Senate approves." Furthermore, Nixon added, he regarded the rule that prevented limitation of debate on rules changes unconstitutional because it interfered with the Senate's "right to make its own rules." No vote was taken, however, on Nixon's advisory opinion, and the cloture rule remained unchanged.

In 1959, Senate liberals proposed that cloture be invoked by a three-fifths majority rather than the unattainable two-thirds, but their motion was badly defeated. Instead, the Senate, under the leadership of Majority Leader Lyndon Johnson, voted seventy-seven to twenty-two to return to the earlier cloture rule, abandoned a decade earlier. Cloture could now be invoked by a two-thirds majority of those present and voting and could be used to limit debate on changes in the rules. The Senate was back where it had started.

What the debate over cloture should tell us is how strongly the Senate prizes its right to discuss and to deliberate, even when that right is exercised by a small minority of senators opposed to issues the majority supports. Public opinion might regard the Senate as distant and unresponsive, Vice-Presidents and Presidents could grow impatient with its ability to obstruct and impede their legislative programs, and liberal senators could condemn the filibuster, but still the Senate stuck by its tradition of free debate. In 1969, Vice-President Hubert Humphrey, by a simple parliamentary maneuver, offered the Senate the chance to change its cloture rule by a simple majority vote. It turned him down, forty-five to fifty-three.

IV

ANOTHER PROBLEM addressed by Congress in this period was the personal conduct of individual senators and representatives and their use of power. In Article I, Section 5, the Constitution had provided that "Each house may determine the rules of its proceedings, punish its members for disorderly behavior, and, with the concurrence of two thirds, expel a member." Neither the House nor the Senate, however, had developed a written code of ethics to govern the behavior of its members. Instead, they had relied on custom and tradition to control personal morality. On occasion, representatives and senators had been censured for misbehavior—such as the Oakes Dawes case mentioned in the first chapter—but in other instances questionable activities had been overlooked and ignored, in spite of public outcry and condemnation.

Several disagreeable incidents in the 1950s and 1960s, however, caused Congress to take a hard look at its lack of specific ethical standards and to demand a higher level of behavior from its members. The first involved the flagrant misuse of power by two congressional committees, the House Un-American Activities Committee and the Senate Permanent Investigations Subcommittee, which exploited their authority to browbeat and intimidate witnesses and to conduct relentless searches for "subversive elements" in American society. The others involved violations of law by individual members of Congress, including Representative Adam Clayton Powell (Democrat, New York), Senator Thomas Dodd (Democrat, Connecticut), and Bobby Baker, the secretary to the Senate majority.

In 1938, the House of Representatives established a committee to investigate "un-American" activities. Its purpose was to check the progress of communism and other forms of radicalism in the United States and to keep these elements out of the American government. The problem with the committee, however, was that it never bothered to define what was meant by "un-American," so that the definition of "un-American" came to be what the chairman or the majority of the committee wanted it to be.

Under the chairmanship of men like Harold Velde (Republican, Illinois), the committee rapidly gained a reputation for dramatic and often tension-filled hearings that made newspaper headlines throughout the country. It spent millions of dollars, produced many volumes of reports, and absorbed many hours of valuable time, but came up with no information about subversive activities that was not already known by the Department of Justice.

In the Senate, the investigation of subversion became the obsession of Senator Joseph McCarthy (Republican, Wisconsin).

McCarthy's chief target seemed to be communists, but it came to include American liberals and leftists of all varieties. During "twenty years of treason," he declared on one occasion, the Democrats, under Franklin Roosevelt and Truman, "conspired" to turn the United States over to the communists. At a speech in Wheeling, West Virginia, in 1950, McCarthy said that he had a list of 205 names of important state department employees who were active, "card-carrying" members of the American Communist party. These employees, he added, were part of a well-organized communist plot to subvert the American government and turn it over to Moscow.

McCarthy used his position as chairman of the Permanent Investigations Subcommittee to further his campaign against subversion. He accused General Marshall, a World War II hero, and Dean Acheson, the secretary of state, of treason and said that President Eisenhower was "weak on communism." He charged that an important expert on Far Eastern affairs at the Johns Hopkins University was the director of the American communist conspiracy. All of these charges were false, but McCarthy was nevertheless able to destroy the careers of many government officials, more than 6,900 of whom were purged during this period. By 1953, he had expanded his investigation to include the Voice of America, the Department of the Army, and other agencies. Many Washington observers concluded that McCarthy used his dramatic methods simply to gain notoriety and fame, but the cold war climate caused many others to wonder if the senator might be right and the country actually in danger from communist infiltration in government affairs.

The House of Representatives was the first to act against the excesses of these committees. In 1952, Speaker Sam Rayburn limited the power of the Un-American Activities Committee by banning all radio, television, or film coverage of any committee hearings. Rayburn based his decision on his reading of House rules, which, he said, offered no authority for coverage of committee activities by these media.

Two years later, in 1954, the House Rules Committee took up the question of committee standards of behavior, and in March, 1955, the House accepted ten new rules designed to place greater control on the conduct of committees and committee chairmen. Among these rules was a provision that required the presence of two members before a committee could conduct business—a direct blow at the chairman of the Un-American Activities Committee who had frequently conducted investigations of witnesses by himself. Other new rules allowed witnesses at hearings to be accompanied by lawyers and barred the release of any evidence given in closed sessions without the consent of the committee. In addition, committees were directed to receive any testimony that might incriminate an individual in closed session and to permit the accused individual to appear before the committee on his own behalf and to subpoena others who might testify on his behalf.

As early as 1950, a Senate committee chaired by Millard Tydings (Democrat, Maryland) had looked into McCarthy's charges against government officials. These charges, the committee had concluded, were "a fraud and a hoax perpetrated on the Senate of the United States and on the American people. They represent perhaps the most nefarious campaign of half-truth and untruth in the history of the Republic." At the time, however, McCarthy was at the height of his power. The Senate largely ignored the conclusion of the committee and when Tydings went up for reelection soon afterward, he was defeated in a campaign where right wing support—drummed up by Senator McCarthy—for a different candidate played an important part.

It was when McCarthy began his investigation of the Department of the Army, which was televised in the spring of 1954, that the Senate began to move against him. A select subcommittee was chosen to draw up charges against him, and in a special Senate session following the elections of 1954, he was censured by a vote of sixty-seven to twenty-two. The censure charged him with failure to cooperate with the Subcommittee on Privileges and Elections in 1952 and with the select committee that had been appointed to look into his activities. Senator McCarthy, it concluded, had "acted contrary to senatorial ethics and tended to bring the Senate into dishonor and disrepute, to obstruct the constitutional processes of the Senate, and to impair its dignity. And such conduct is hereby condemned."

McCarthy continued to serve in the Senate, but his power had been broken. The Senate failed to adopt an overall set of rules to govern committee behavior, but left these rules up to each individual committee. Those adopted by the Permanent Investigations Subcommittee, McCarthy's former committee now under the chairmanship of John McClellan (Democrat, Arkansas), were very similar to the rules earlier adopted by the House of Representatives.

Further strengthening of House and Senate rules regarding the personal behavior of representatives and senators came in the 1960s after the outbreak of fresh scandals. The first came in 1963 and involved Bobby Baker, secretary to the Democrats in the Senate and close friend and associate of Lyndon Johnson, the former majority leader who had become Vice-President under President John Kennedy. Baker was regarded as the Senate's "most powerful employee" and was well known for his thorough knowledge of the Senate's inner workings.

The charges against Baker were numerous, but boiled down to the accusation that he had used his position for personal gain. Indeed, Baker had become a rich man, far richer than his salary would allow by exploiting his familiarity with Senate ways to advance his own business interests. After these disclosures had become public, the Senate gave the Rules and Administration Committee responsibility for looking into Baker's activities. The committee—dominated by a Democratic majority—accused the former Senate employee, who had resigned under pressure, of "many gross improprieties," but made no mention of any actual violation of law. Republicans charged that the report was a "whitewash," and subsequent events bore them out. Later, Baker was convicted in court and imprisoned for income tax evasion, theft, and conspiracy to defraud the government.

In response to the Baker scandal, the Senate established the Select Committee on Standards and Conduct. The committee's purpose was to investigate accusations of misconduct by senators and Senate employees, to propose the kind of disciplinary action that should be taken against individuals convicted of the charges against them, and to decide upon a code of conduct to govern the behavior of senators. No Senate committee had previously been charged with these specific tasks.

In 1966, the committee made its first inquiry. Thomas Dodd, member of a prominent Connecticut family and highly regarded as a senator, had been accused by a nationally syndicated newspaper columnist of misuse of campaign funds. Dodd at first denied the accusations, but when the Committee on Standards and Conduct issued its report to the Senate, it recommended that he be censured not only for misuse of political campaign money, but also for double-billing the government for official and private travel. The Senate accepted the first charge by a vote of ninety-two to five and rejected the second fifty-one to forty-five. The censure helped to destroy Dodd's reputation in his home state, and he was defeated for reelection in 1970.

Meanwhile, an additional scandal and controversy had been brewing in the House of Representatives. Adam Clayton Powell had long been deeply resented by his fellow representatives for his flamboyance and extravagant manner. First elected to the House in 1945 from New York City's Harlem, he had become, through the process of seniority, chairman of the important Education and Labor Committee. One of the few blacks in Congress, he might have come to play a more significant and useful role in the House if he had been willing to pay greater attention to House customs and traditions and devote more time to his committee's activities.

But Powell had problems. In 1958, he had been indicted for income tax evasion and later paid $28,000 in back taxes and penalties to the government. Sued for libel in 1960, he was held in contempt of court by the judge in the case on several occasions. These incidents alone gave him a certain amount of notoriety and earned him the criticism of his fellow representatives and the press. But it was the fact that he kept his wife on the Senate payroll at $20,000, although she lived in Puerto Rico, as well as his frequent trips at public expense and his dictatorial and erratic methods as committee chairman, that led to his downfall.

In 1967, the caucus of the Democratic party members in the House voted to deprive Representative Powell of his committee chairmanship. The revolt against him had been led by members of his own committee. Subsequently, the House voted 365 to 65 to deny him his seat in Congress until a select committee could investigate his activities and issue a report. The report recommended that Powell be censured for gross misconduct, deprived of his seniority, and fined $40,000 for "misuse of public funds," but that he be allowed to keep the seat to which he had been duly elected.

The whole House, however, was of a different mind, and on March 1, 1967, it voted to declare his seat vacant and to refuse him admission to Congress as a representative. For the next two years, Powell carried his case through the federal district courts to the Supreme Court, where he won a seven-to-one decision in his favor. The high court, in an opinion handed down by Chief Justice Earl Warren, declared that Powell had been improperly excluded by the House and directed that he be readmitted. The House submitted to the ruling, but fined the Harlem congressman $25,000 and stripped him of his seniority.

As a result of the furor over the Baker, Dodd, and Powell cases, both houses of Congress adopted strict codes of behavior in 1968. In the House of Representatives, the code was drawn up by the Committee on Standards of Official Behavior, and in the Senate, by the Select Committee on Standards and Conduct. The House Code of Official Conduct, as it came to be called, required members to keep campaign funds separate from personal funds and forbade any House member or employee to use his or her official position as a means to receive improper compensation. Other provisions placed a limit on the value of gifts representatives could receive from lobbyists and obligated House staff to perform the work for which they were paid. At the time it adopted the new code of ethics, the House also passed a new rule that required members to disclose outside financial interests each year to the Committee on Official Conduct. This information was to be made available to the public.

The new code of conduct adopted by the Senate required a full accounting of campaign contributions and limited the use to which they could be put. It likewise required senators and their most important aides to file detailed financial statements each year with the Select Committee on Standards and Behavior. These financial statements were to remain privileged, however, and senators were required to make public only gifts of $50 or more and honoraria of $300 or more. The Select Committee was given the power to investigate possible financial misconduct on the part of a senator, but only after that senator had been warned that he was being investigated and given the chance to reply to the charges against him in closed session.

The new codes of conduct adopted by the House and Senate were extraordinary in many ways. They revealed a deep concern that ethical standards be established and followed, and they showed that Congress was troubled by its public image. Yet rigid as the new codes seemed on paper, they did not do away with congressional misconduct. There were still too many loopholes that provided a means of escape from censure, if a member of Congress was inclined to use these loopholes. The Senate had rejected a proposal for full *public* disclosure of finances, for instance, and this cast doubt on the seriousness of its reforms. In 1969, Senator Clifford Case (Republican, New Jersey) told his colleagues that full confidence in Congress could be established only through a rigid code of behavior strictly adhered to by every member of the House and Senate. Public confidence, he implied, could be won only if senators and representatives were willing to prove, as far as possible, that they had no personal interests that would benefit from their positions as members of Congress.

V

IN THE years after World War II, Congress had advanced on several fronts. The Legislative Reorganization Act of 1946 had altered the committee structure of both the House and the Senate. Changes had been made in the House Rules Committee and attempted against the filibuster in the Senate. Both houses had adopted new codes of ethical conduct and placed restrictions on the abuse of power by committees and committee chairmen. At the time these changes were taking place, however, other more subtle changes were taking place whose effect was noted only later.

The most important of the changes was the transformation in House and Senate membership and in the leadership that guided both.

Between the 1950s and the 1970s the average age of a representative dropped considerably, so that by 1977 it had fallen to below fifty for the first time since World War II. In addition, the same period saw a marked decrease in the number of House members who had served for long periods of time. The newer, younger representatives tended to be more liberal than their earlier counterparts and less likely to be bound by tradition and custom. They also tended to be more individualistic, refusing to be guided by party loyalty and discipline.

In the Senate, too, change seemed to play into the hands of the liberals. Since 1958, the Senate has been dominated by Democrats, with the number of Democratic senators never falling below fifty-five. Moreover, the number of conservative Democrats from the South declined, while the number of Democrats from other parts of the country continued to rise. Gone were the days when southerners who had served for long periods of time seemed to control Senate activities. Power now passed to a new group of senators, with new interests and concerns and different ideas of how the country should be governed.

The changes in House and Senate leadership were no less striking. The House of the 1950s had been characterized by its powerful Speaker, Sam Rayburn. Rayburn's motto, which was told to every new representative, was "To get along, go along": play by the rules, accept custom, don't rock the boat, and you will slowly rise to power and influence. When Rayburn died in 1961, he was replaced by John McCormack (Democrat, Massachusetts), a far less effective man, who allowed the powers of the speakership to erode. When he was replaced in 1970 by Carl Albert (Democrat, Oklahoma), liberals at last had a Speaker who would not oppose demands for change. Whereas Rayburn had stood by custom and tradition and had dominated the House by the force of his personality and his enormous political skills, Albert believed in consensus politics and in arriving at compromises on issues through discussion and deliberation.

During the same period, the leadership of the majority in the Senate passed from Lyndon Johnson, the close friend of Sam Rayburn, to Mike Mansfield (Democrat, Montana). Johnson had centralized power in the Senate around himself and controlled the Democratic Party Conference with an iron hand. He was an aggressive majority leader who did not hesitate to make his personal opinions felt and to exert his will. New senators went to him if they expected to gain influence in the Senate.

Mansfield was a very different kind of man. He was a careful organizer and manager, who believed his most important duty as majority leader was to see that the Senate moved smoothly and in an orderly fashion to conduct its business. Where Johnson attempted to influence the outcome of every bill, Mansfield was prone to leave decisions up to individual senators. Mansfield likewise made an effort to bring new members into committee positions where they could exercise authority and responsibility and to appoint liberal senators to positions of prominence.

The period in congressional history after 1946, then, can be seen as a prelude to the major reforms of the 1970s, which are the subject of the next chapter. The Legislative Reorganization Act of 1946 had tackled some of the House and Senate's more pressing problems, but had left others unsolved. The power of the House Rules Committee had been tamed, but filibustering still tied up Senate business. Even this period's most lasting contribution—the new codes of ethics adopted by both houses—had faults, which some critics said needed to be remedied. But further change was in the air. Changes in House and Senate membership and leadership had given Congress a new, more liberal complexion. The new Congress would attempt two tasks in the 1970s. First, it would continue to try to complete the modernization of congressional rules and procedures begun in 1946 and, second, it would confront the growing power of the imperial presidency in order to restore the traditional balance of power between Congress and the executive branch.

CHAPTER SEVEN

CONGRESS REFORMS ITSELF

Congressional reform in general means nothing less than the overall revitalization of the legislative branch of the United States government, a reconstruction of the House and Senate through discard of anachronistic practices, and the adoption of twentieth-century procedures and utilization of contemporary techniques, to enable the Congress to effectively perform for modern-day America—Bruce R. Hopkins, lawyer and author

THE 1970s witnessed two kinds of reform in Congress. The first was the result of bipartisan efforts including both Democrats and Republicans that led to basic reforms of the House and Senate. The second type was reform in party structure and rules undertaken independently by each party in the House caucuses and the Senate conferences. Because the Democrats overwhelmingly dominated both houses of Congress, their reforms were regarded as more significant and influential, but reforms in the Republican party were likewise important and should not be underemphasized.

Both kinds of reform, however, endeavored to establish the

same objectives. These objectives included the need to modernize House and Senate practices, to make Congress more responsive to public needs, and to spread power and authority in both houses so that more senators and representatives shared in the decision-making process. The purpose of the reform diverged only when it came to party interests. Democratic liberals sought changes that would enhance their position in the Democratic party, whereas Republicans looked for changes that would strengthen their party's minority position in Congress. But even these politically motivated reforms revealed a desire to abandon tradition and accept new ways of doing things.

I

IN 1966, a new legislative reorganization bill designed to supplement and improve the reforms of 1946 was introduced in the House of Representatives by Ray Madden (Democrat, Indiana) and in the Senate by Mike Monroney. Twenty years before, Monroney, as a member of the House, had been one of the key men responsible for the earlier Reorganization Act. In 1968, the new bill, which had bipartisan support, died in the House Rules Committee, but two years later it was revived and passed both the House and Senate in 1970.

The new act stressed the need for greater openness in committee affairs and improved the status of minority party members. In both houses, all committees were now obligated to publish roll-call votes, and in the House, where representatives had frequently concealed their votes on bills in committee and thereby evaded the possible anger of their constituents, votes were now registered by the name of the representative.

Minority members of committees were given the right to call witnesses of their own to committee hearings in addition to the witnesses called by the majority party. Moreover, the minority was granted permission to file minority or supplementary reports on legislation opposing the majority report. Other provisions required committees to have open and written rules and allowed committee members to call committee meetings without the approval of the chairman. All committee members had to be given advance notice of committee meetings and could call up a bill that had been cleared by the committee for floor action but was being withheld by the chairman.

Rules were also changed to limit the membership of senators to two major committees and one minor committee, either select or joint. No senator could serve on more than one of the central committees—Armed Services, Appropriations, Finance, or Foreign Relations. Similarly, no senator could hold the chairmanship of more than one full committee and one subcommittee of a major committee. This was done to keep one senator from amassing too much power, to free senators from time-consuming commitments, and to enable them to concentrate their ability in one or two areas of importance.

Finally, the Reorganization Act of 1970 made provisions to give the House and Senate more information on government finances, an attack on the habit of secrecy practiced by the executive branch, and established a Joint Committee on Congressional Operations. This committee, made up of Democrats and Republicans, senators and representatives, was charged with keeping an eye on new problems that arose and to study older problems that still needed solution.

The new Reorganization Act made no attempt to solve the problem of filibustering in the Senate. But it did make an indirect attack on seniority by giving committee members the power to call meetings and to move legislation to the floor of Congress over the wishes of powerful chairmen. Perhaps the most important provisions of the act were its improvement of the rights of minority committee members, its call for greater openness in committee voting, and the creation of the Joint Committee on Congressional Operations. The creation of the committee was proof that Congress was not fully satisfied with its reforms and that it was willing to provide a means for ongoing change.

II

MEANWHILE, LIBERAL Democrats in the House of Representatives had found a different means to bring about reform. Although liberal Democrats formed a majority of their party in the House in the late 1960s, they held few key positions and were unable to exercise power according to their weight in numbers. The one way out of this dilemma was to gain control of the Democratic party apparatus in the House, now largely dominated by a few tradition-bound conservatives.

But how could they gain control of the party apparatus? Many liberal House members began to turn their attention to the Democratic party caucus. For years, the caucus had been little more than a formality, meeting every two years at the beginning of each new Congress to accept the nominations for chairmanships and committee membership made by the Democratic Committee on Committees. The caucus served merely as a rubber stamp for the conservative Democratic leadership. If the liberals could revitalize the caucus, however, and come to dominate its activities, they could reform Democratic practice and policy in the House.

In 1969, the members of the Democratic Study Group (DSG), an organization of liberal House Democrats, along with Majority Leader Carl Albert, pressured Speaker John McCormack into supporting the activation of the party caucus. A new party rule was established that required a meeting of the caucus once every month if fifty members demanded the meeting in writing and placed a petition before the caucus chairman that outlined a proposed agenda for the meeting.

Armed with this rule, the liberals were prepared to press for further reform. At a meeting of the caucus in March, 1970, they proposed that a committee be established to study problems of party organization in the House. The proposal was accepted and the caucus chairman, Representative Dan Rostenkowski of Illinois, appointed Julia Butler Hansen of Washington to chair the new committee. The committee was officially named the Committee on Organization, Study, and Review, but it is more often known as the Hansen committee.

The first Hansen committee report appeared in 1971 and was quickly adopted by the party caucus. The report offered two reforms that were a direct attack on seniority. First, the Committee on Committees was told that it still had the right to appoint committee chairmen and members, but that it need not follow the practice of seniority in making its nominations. But more important, the first Hansen report changed the method of approving committee nominations in the caucus. Previously the caucus had voted for a whole slate of appointments made by the Committee on Committees, a method that assured that the caucus would accept the nominations of the party leadership.

Now, however, under the Hansen reforms, the caucus would vote on the nominations *one committee at a time*, thus making it easier to reject individual appointments. A second reform limited legislative subcommittee chairmanships to one per representative and gave each subcommittee chairman the right to appoint one professional staff member to assist the subcommittee.

On the same day that the Democrats adopted the Hansen proposals, the House Republican conference, the Republican equivalent of the Democratic caucus, accepted a new rule that permitted Republican representatives to vote by secret ballot on that party's nominations for committee chairmanships—a method of voting that assured that representatives would not be punished if they voted against senior Republicans. Both parties now had at their disposal a means of challenging the seniority system and of undermining the authority of powerful chairmen.

At the beginning of 1973, the Hansen committee brought out a second series of proposals. These proposals further altered the way in which committee appointments were made by requiring that *each* nomination by the Committee on Committees be voted on automatically, rather than committee by committee as the first Hansen report had required. Furthermore, the size of the Committee on Committees was expanded. Earlier it had been composed entirely of the Democratic members of the Ways and Means Committee, but now it would include the Speaker of the House, the majority leader, and the Democratic caucus chairman. Instead of the chairman of Ways and Means, the Speaker would head the committee. This took the power over the Committee on Committees out of the hands of the chairman of Ways and Means and turned it over to the House Democratic leadership.

The second series of Hansen proposals also created a new Democratic Steering and Policy Committee, chaired by the Speaker and composed of twenty-four members. Its duty would be to direct the party's legislative strategy in the House. In order to facilitate the passage of legislation, the Hansen report offered a means by which the system of "closed rules" could be fought. Under closed rules, a committee could introduce a bill to the House floor to which no amendments could be considered, thus preventing meaningful change in the bill. The Hansen report proposed that fifty or more Democrats could demand that a bill under closed rules be considered by the caucus and if the caucus approved, the bill would then have to face the possibility of amendment on the House floor.

Another section of the second Hansen report dealt with the problems of subcommittees and was known as the "subcommittee bill of rights." It took the power to appoint subcommittee chairmen away from the chairman of the committee of which the subcommittee was a part and gave this power of appointment to the Democratic members of the committee as a whole. Each committee member was likewise given the right to at least one "choice subcommittee assignment" to assure that no member was slighted or denied a position of some importance. Other provisions of the Hansen subcommittee bill of rights required that each subcommittee should have fixed areas of jurisdiction in order to prevent overlapping of responsibility, granted subcommittees adequate budgets and staff, and required a subcommittee ratio of Democrats and Republicans that was similar to the party ratio of the parent committee.

The third set of Hansen reforms came out the next year, in 1974, and contained two principal sections. The first granted more power to the Speaker of the House by giving him greater control over bills. He could now send a bill to more than one committee for consideration or divide a single bill into parts and send those parts to different committees. The second required that Congress return to Washington each election year in December before the new session began in January. This gave a month's time to the members of each party in which to organize and prepare for the next Congress, thus strengthening the role the Democratic caucus and the Republican conference would play in congressional affairs.

When the first Democratic caucus met under the new rule in December, 1974, it added two more important reforms to the ones already instituted. The power to make committee appointments was entirely removed from the Ways and Means Committee and given to the new Democratic Steering and Policy Committee. Furthermore, if the caucus rejected the nominations for committee posts made by the Steering and Policy Committee, new nominations would then be made from the floor of the caucus, giving individual representatives the chance to name committee chairmen.

The three Hansen reports had two general effects on the House. The reforms made between 1970 and 1973 were primarily designed to make the House more democratic by changing the committee system. Subcommittees were strengthened and power decentralized within the standing committees. Since the number of subcommittees was far greater than the number of committees, this meant that a larger number of House members could assume positions of influence and power by chairing subcommittees. Power was now shared by a large number of representatives rather than held by a few senior members as it had been in earlier Congresses.

But if the reforms of 1970 to 1973 favored democratization and decentralization of power, the reforms of 1973 to 1975 went in the opposite direction. These latter reforms can be seen as an effort to concentrate more power in the hands of the Speaker and the party caucus. The revitalized caucus now had an influence and authority over party affairs it had lacked for many decades, while the Speaker had greater control over the flow of legislation. The first Hansen reforms had given each House member greater equality and responsibility, but then had sought to balance that equality and responsibility with a stronger party leadership that could provide order and stability and guidance when they were needed. The dangers of decentralization—too little party unity and too much individualism on the part of House members—were canceled by a renewed centralization of authority.

III

MANY OF the reforms passed by the House of Representatives and the Democratic caucus in this period had the support of a new and recent phenomenon in Washington political life, the public interest lobbies. The most important of these lobbies included John Gardner's Common Cause and Ralph Nader's Congress Project, but there was also help from longer established political organizations like the League of Women Voters of the United States and the Americans for Democratic Action. These groups lobbied tirelessly for changes that would improve the responsiveness of Congress to public needs and frequently issued reports * that made specific suggestions for reform. Because of their activities, these groups played a significant role in the creation of the new Congress.

In addition to the reforms already mentioned, the House made other changes in its procedures in the 1970s. The year 1973 saw the adoption of a new bill further emphasizing openness and responsibility. Known as House Resolution 259, the bill passed by an overwhelming vote of 370 to 27 and required that all committee and subcommittee sessions be open to the press and public unless a majority of the committee's or subcommittee's members voted to close a particular session by a roll-call vote. Closed hearings could take place only when public disclosure would endanger national security or violate House rules. The new openness rule drastically altered the practices of House committees and subcommittees. In 1972, the year before the rule was passed, forty-four percent of committee and subcommittee meetings were closed to the public. By 1975, this had dropped to fewer than three percent.

The desire for openness likewise led the House to reconsider its position on television and radio coverage of House activities. In 1950, Speaker Rayburn had outlawed radio and television

* These reports were sometimes deeply resented by Congress, however, because they were often critical of the House and Senate. This was especially true of Nader's Congress Project, which, on at least one occasion, issued a report deemed "totally inaccurate and misleading" by many senators and representatives.

coverage of the Un-American Activities Committee so that the committee would not continue to make a spectacle of itself. In 1970, however, the House amended its rules to permit coverage of committee hearings, but at the same time adopted a rigid set of standards that were to govern broadcasting in the House. The purposes of the hearings to be aired were not to be distorted, nor were the broadcasts in any way to cast aspersions on the House or upon its members or committees.

It was the Watergate affair that helped to overcome the aversion many representatives still had to radio and television coverage. The broadcast media were permitted to cover the House Judiciary Committee's hearings on the impeachment of Richard Nixon. The public reaction to the televised hearings—during which the members of the Judiciary Committee conducted themselves with intelligence and responsibility—was so favorable that other committees began to allow coverage of their activities. Most striking perhaps were the televised hearings the Appropriations Committee permitted of its investigation of CIA activities in 1975.

Later in the 1970s, the House began to consider proposals to allow television cameras to cover sessions on the House floor. This led to the first television coverage of the whole House in action in 1978, a step that was taken cautiously, since many representatives feared that the presence of the cameras would lead some members to dominate activities in order to be seen throughout the country. The use of television on the House floor, however, is still too new and untried for anyone to make a judgment of its effect on House customs and procedures.*

Further concern for the improvement of ethical standards was likewise manifested by the House in the 1970s, with the passage

* Modern electronic technology did, however, make one distinct contribution to the House during this time. In 1973, the House installed an electronic voting system that made voting by the 435 representatives a speedier process.

of two new bills in 1971 and 1974. The first bill tightened disclosure requirements on campaign contributions and other income and required members of Congress to report their expenditures during a campaign. The role that labor unions and corporations—two sources of large sums of money and therefore of possible corruption—could play in campaigns were also defined and limited. The 1974 law established limits on political contributions and spending in federal elections.

The House Committee on Standards of Official Conduct continued to oversee the activities of Congressmen, but only occasionally used its power of investigation. In 1978 and 1979, it looked into charges against Representative Charles Diggs (Democrat, Michigan) and found evidence that he had illegally diverted government funds for his own use. Diggs was later convicted in court and may serve time in prison. Recently the House has censured Representative Charles Wilson (Democrat, California), for irregularities involving campaign financing. In addition, the FBI has uncovered information that has led to the indictment of at least two Representatives for questionable activities. The names of several other members of the House and one prominent Senator have been mentioned in the FBI case.

Another important bill passed in this period was House Resolution 988, which required every standing committee except Appropriations to establish oversight subcommittees. The purpose of the oversight subcommittees was to provide close supervision of congressional agencies in order to see if legislation passed by Congress has been carried into effect. For the first time in history, committees now had a means systematically to examine the results of legislation and to see if that legislation achieved the ends it had been designed to produce.

On one occasion in the 1970s, however, the House of Representatives rejected a proposal that offered significant reforms. These proposals were put forth by the House Select Committee on Committees, a bipartisan group made up of Democrats and Republicans of varying political ideologies. The Select Committee on Committees was also known as the Bolling committee, after its chairman, Richard Bolling (Democrat, Missouri), a longtime advocate of House reorganization.

The report issued by the Bolling committee in 1974, after it had held extensive hearings on reform, was revolutionary. It called for a drastic alteration of the committee system by a realignment of committee jurisdictions. It sought to reduce duplication of committee work and overlapping of responsibilities by eliminating some committees and reorganizing others. In addition, it stipulated that each representative could be a member of only one major committee.

The Bolling report had much to recommend it. It would have achieved the aims of many congressional reformers by streamlining House machinery and by providing more time for each representative to concentrate on one area of expertise. Furthermore, it had the approval of conservatives as well as liberals, Republicans as well as Democrats. But the Bolling report stepped on too many toes. It alienated many committee chairmen who feared that its proposals, if adopted, would destroy their committees or diminish their power. The report also alienated many Democrats, because they believed it gave too much power to the Republican minority. One Democratic leader spoke for his fellow Democrats when he reminded them that they had experienced heavy-handed treatment when the Republicans were in the majority and that now was not the time to give the other party powers it would never have granted the Democrats. The House rejected the Bolling report, not even bringing it up for a final vote.

Nevertheless, the new House that emerged from the reforms of the 1970s was a very different institution from the House of a decade earlier. As a result of the Legislative Reorganization Act of 1970, the Hansen committee reports, and the other reforms of the 1970s, the importance of subcommittees was on the rise, the power and influence of committee chairmen was in decline, and the practice of seniority had been crippled. During the same period, the Democratic members of the House and to a lesser extent the Republicans had transformed the party caucus from an organization with little real responsibility into one that played an integral part in the decision-making process in the House.

In 1955, there had been eighty-three standing subcommittees in the House. By 1974, there were 139, an increase of more than sixty-seven percent. But more important, the subcommittees of the mid-1970s had been given the staff, resources, and jurisdiction that allowed them greater independence of activity and removed them from absolute control of committee chairmen. Subcommittee chairmanships were now attractive positions for ambitious representatives to hold and, because there were so many of them, the talents and abilities of a greater number of representatives could be brought to bear on the legislative process.

The rise of subcommittee government inevitably entailed the decline of the committee chairmen. Between 1970 and 1975, as a result of the Hansen reforms, committee chairmen lost their power to appoint subcommittee chairmen, to decide which subcommittee would consider legislation, and to prevent subcommittees from holding meetings. Moreover, they no longer had the authority to determine the number of subcommittees their committee would have or the right to specify their size or majority party membership.

By 1976, several of the most powerful committee chairmen had been removed from office. Wilbur Mills, Chairman of Ways and Means, and Wayne Hays, Chairman of the House Administration Committee, lost their positions because of scandals they were involved in. Edward Hébert (Democrat, Louisiana) of the Armed Services Committee, Wright Patman (Democrat, Texas) of Banking and Currency, and Bob Poage (Democrat, Texas) of the

Agriculture Committee were removed from their chairmanships by the revitalized Democratic caucus, which voted them out. Hébert, Patman, and Poage had each served more than thirty years in the House. In their places, the caucus put chairmen of its own choosing.

The decrease in the amount of power exercised by committee chairmen and the removal of several of the older men who had headed committees helped to undermine seniority, but did not wipe it out. The caucus still tended to choose men and women on the basis of age and experience in the House and to place them in positions of importance. But the basic structure of seniority had been changed. Now that chairmen exercised less authority, it was less important who held the position of chairman. After the reforms of the 1970s, no chairman held absolute power, but had to defer to the opinions of the members of his committee, the subcommittee chairmen, and the Democratic caucus.

Along with the importance of subcommittees and the decline of committee chairmen, the emergence of "party government" was the third characteristic of the new House. Party government in this case, however, did not mean old-fashioned party loyalty and discipline. What it meant was that the Democratic party caucus had been strengthened as a tool to be used in the production of legislation and the development of party policy. Democratic party activists—for the most part liberals—could now use caucus to attain ends they could not achieve through parliamentary maneuvers on the House floor. By turning problems and issues over to the caucus for consideration and acceptance, they overcame the coalition of conservative Democrats and Republicans that so frequently had blocked liberal and moderate legislation in committees or in the House.

In addition to the revitalized party caucus, the strengthened House leadership and the new Steering and Policy Committee helped to further the cause of party government. The Speaker now played an important role in the selection of committee chairmen and members and could implement his party's legislative program more directly and fruitfully. The Steering and Policy Committee, on the other hand, could act to restrain and guide the Speaker and keep him working along lines already established by the party. In short, the new powers granted the Speaker were not his to use personally, but as an instrument of his party.

IV

ONE OF the most important new powers exercised by the Speaker was his power to name all the Democratic members of the House Rules Committee, subject to the approval of the Democratic caucus. His power was enhanced by the fact that the Democratic members of the committee were subject to reappointment at the beginning of each new Congress, thus giving the Speaker and the caucus the right to remove individuals who proved uncooperative. These new procedures involving the Rules Committee made it impossible for the chairman of the committee to obstruct or destroy legislation that he or she personally disliked, as chairmen of the Rules Committee had done in the past.

The reduction of the powers of the Rules Committee chairman, however, did not destroy the importance of the committee. It still had the power to decide how bills would move to the House floor, and it could control the flow of legislation. What had changed was the role it played in these activities and the methods it used to carry out its responsibilities.

According to political scientist Bruce Oppenheimer, the committee now functions as a legislative "traffic cop," as a "field commander" for the majority and minority leaderships in the House, and as a "dress rehearsal" for legislation before it goes on to the House floor. As traffic cop, the committee performs a duty similar to the role played by earlier Rules Committees. Although it now rarely destroys legislation, it does on occasion delay a bill in order to improve its chances of passage or if it receives a request for delay from the House leadership.

In its role as traffic cop, the Rules Committee also helps to settle jurisdiction disputes that arise among committees and subcommittees. These disputes involve the question of which committee or subcommittee has the right to consider a given bill. Because committee jurisdictions are jealously guarded and jurisdictional disputes can arouse anger on the part of a committee that feels slighted when denied the right to consider a bill it believes to be under its jurisdiction, the traffic cop role of the Rules Committee can be very important.

As field commander, the Rules Committee functions as an arm of the House leadership. If the leadership dislikes a bill or believes that certain legislation has problems that need to be ironed out before final passage, the Rules Committee will act to slow down the bill until it has the approval of the leadership. As traffic cop, then, the committee makes decisions for the House membership as a whole, Democrats and Republicans. As field commander, it responds solely to the desires of the majority party leadership.

In its role as a dress rehearsal for legislation, the Rules Committee serves as a microcosm of what will happen later in the macrocosm of the House. By attending a session of the Rules Committee or of one of its subcommittees, an observer can hear the arguments that will be made on both sides of the issue when it is later presented to the House. The floor manager of a bill can learn a great deal from his or her experience before the Rules Committee. The experience will show where the chief opposition lies and what the opponents' position is. The floor manager will likewise learn about the strengths and weaknesses of the bill and be able to amend those weaknesses before taking the bill before the House. And since the Rules Committee is representative of the Congress—with liberals, moderates, and conservatives represented by able spokesmen—floor managers can gain a rough estimate of how their bills will fare when put to a House vote. Opposition from both moderates and conservatives, for instance, will probably guarantee defeat, whereas moderate and liberal support in the Rules Committee will indicate a better chance of passage.

In its role as dress rehearsal for legislation, the Rules Committee can also work to make or break congressional reputations. Supporters of bills are expected to display expertise and complete understanding of their bill and its ramifications. If a supporter of a bill presents a poor case for the bill before the Rules Committee, he or she will more than likely lose the case and earn a reputation for carelessness or lack of ability, while a good case will earn a representative the respect and esteem of colleagues.

Moreover, since members of the Rules Committee are the first in the House to hear the arguments on bills, other House members tend to use them as sources of information. It is not unusual for Rules Committee members to receive questions and telephone calls from other representatives about new bills, putting additional pressure on sponsors of bills to give adequate summaries of their legislation before the Rules Committee so that the word goes out to the rest of the House that the bill is a good bill and that it has an able and informed sponsor.

V

THE 1970s also brought important changes to Senate practices and procedures. If these changes were less dramatic and striking than the changes experienced by the House of Representatives, it was because the Senate was already a more open institution than the House, with fewer problems to solve. The Senate had no tradition of closed rules that had to be overcome; it adhered to the practice of recorded votes so that every senator could be held responsible for the position he or she took on controversial issues. It likewise had opened its activities to coverage by radio and television.

Nevertheless, the reforms of the 1970s in the Senate paralleled those in the House. The Senate reforms challenged the principle of seniority. They stressed the need for greater openness and responsibility, especially in committee activities, and they spread authority among a larger number of senators, giving junior senators a greater part to play in Senate affairs. In addition, a new rule was passed that made it easier to limit debate and control the filibuster.

The first attack on the seniority system came in 1971 when Fred Harris (Democrat, Oklahoma) and Charles Mathias (Republican, Maryland) proposed that a standard of merit be adopted to judge the abilities of senators and to control their advancement in the Senate. Committee chairmen, they suggested, as well as ranking minority committee members, should be nominated by a majority vote of the party caucuses and then elected by a majority vote of the full Senate at the beginning of each new Congress. However, their plan was regarded as too revolutionary and was never brought to the Senate floor for consideration.

Genuine reform in the seniority system was first made by the Republican caucus in 1973 when it accepted a plan under which the Republican members of each committee would elect the ranking minority members of that committee. This made it possible for Republican committee members to choose their leader on the basis of seniority. If they found the senior member undesirable, however, they could bypass him and elect someone else. Two years later, the Democratic caucus altered its rules to require that committee chairmen be forced to face reelection every two years. In addition, the caucus required that chairmen be elected by secret ballot when one-fifth of the caucus so requested, giving Democrats in the Senate the opportunity to vote against powerful committee chairmen without fear of reprisal.

The importance of openness was stressed in legislation passed in 1975. Every committee was now required to keep transcripts or electronic recordings of committee meetings, unless a majority of the committee desired to omit them. All committee meetings were to be public unless a majority voted in open session to close the meeting. However, the committees could vote to close their meetings only under special circumstances that included issues involving national security, discussion of criminal charges that might damage an individual if made public, or any matters that the Senate, by law, was required to keep secret. The openness rules helped to undermine longtime habits of secrecy in the Senate and helped to strengthen the position of newer senators by giving them access to information they would otherwise not be privileged to have. An open Senate was one where power and influence could be shared by larger numbers of senators.

Other measures likewise enhanced the status of the junior members of the Senate. As part of the Legislative Reorganization Act of 1970, the Senate had limited senators to membership on only one of the top four standing committees, Armed Services, Finance, Appropriations, and Foreign Relations. This measure had prevented these committees from saturation by senior senators seeking desirable positions and made it possible for senators with much less experience in the Senate to become members of important and influential committees early in their careers. In 1975, for instance, Gary Hart (Democrat, Colorado), Patrick Leahy (Democrat, Vermont), and John Culver (Democrat, Iowa), each of whom had only recently been elected to the Senate, were assigned to the Armed Services Committee, while two-year Senate members William Hathaway (Democrat, Maine) and Floyd Haskell

(Democrat, Colorado) were assigned to the Finance Committee. Ten years earlier, these assignments of junior senators to senior positions would have been unthinkable.

Moreover, the number of standing committees grew from fifteen to eighteen between 1957 and 1975, and the number of subcommittees grew from 113 to 140. This opened up new positions on which junior senators could serve. In 1975, Senate Resolution 60 allowed junior senators for the first time to hire additional legislative staff to assist them in their committee responsibilities. With additional expertise and professional guidance to aid them in their work, younger senators now had a stronger position from which to challenge the authority of committee chairmen. Taken together, these changes reveal the degree to which power in the Senate had moved from the hands of a few committee chairmen and was now distributed more evenly and democratically.

Every two years between 1959 and 1975, except for 1973, Senate reformers had raised the problem of cloture and the filibuster. In every year but 1975, they failed to get the reforms they desired. Indeed, success came in 1975 only after three weeks of hard debate and after the reformers had agreed to a compromise. They had sought a rule that would invoke cloture by a simple majority of the whole Senate or by three-fifths of those present and voting. They had to settle for a rule in which cloture was invoked by three-fifths of the whole Senate. This meant that filibustering could now be brought to an end by a vote of sixty senators rather than the two-thirds of those present and voting that was previously necessary. Many reformers thought that the new rule was a step in the right direction, but others doubted that it would have any real effect on Senate procedure.

The reforms of the 1970s had created a new Congress whose most striking characteristics were equality and democracy. In the

House and Senate, power and responsibility had been spread more widely, giving larger numbers of representatives and senators "a piece of the action." Members of Congress now shared authority on a more nearly equal basis than in earlier years. Younger and newer representatives and senators could make their influence felt on the legislative process.

The new Congress was also a more open institution than earlier Congresses and one where the practice of seniority played a less important role. Greater openness meant that the press and public had access to committee proceedings from which they had once been barred. It likewise meant that they had a greater fund of knowledge and information on which to judge the performance of individual senators and representatives, the committees, and Congress as a whole. In addition, an open Congress was one in which democracy and equality of membership could play a more important role. The practice of secrecy had played into the hands of a few powerful individuals. With the establishment of openness, these individuals now had public responsibility for what they had once been able to hide behind closed doors.

Greater equality and openness contributed to the decline of seniority. As more representatives and senators began to share a "piece of the action," members of Congress with longer congressional careers behind them lost power that would have been theirs naturally under the old system. In the new Congress, senior members were not disregarded, especially if they had shown talent and ability. It was strict adherence to the policy of seniority that had passed by the way. The days were gone in both houses when a few senior committee members dominated Congress.

This new Congress was characterized by an expanded number of subcommittees and by a larger professional and clerical staff to help representatives and senators carry the increased congressional workload. This was in keeping with the theme of modernization of congressional procedures that had dominated many of the reforms of the 1970s. And in keeping with democracy and equality, subcommittee positions and staff were spread among larger numbers of members of Congress. Even first-year members now had access to expertise and information that would enable them to form considered judgments on issues before the House and Senate.

The Congresses of the 1970s displayed a greater vitality and a stronger spirit of innovation than Congresses had for many years. This vitality and spirit of innovation led to the reforms that made Congress a more democratic and modern institution and played an important part in the other side of congressional change: the restoration of the equal role Congress must play with the President and the executive branch under the Constitution. It is now time to turn to this other side of congressional reform in the 1970s—the confrontation with the imperial presidency and the reassertion of the rights of Congress in our form of government.

CHAPTER EIGHT

CONGRESS CHALLENGES A PRESIDENT

To be honest about it, how one feels about the "inherent" powers of the Presidency has been generally determined throughout our history by how one feels about the use to which they are put and the pressing needs of the time—I. F. Stone, prominent liberal journalist

AFTER 1933, as we have seen, the powers of the presidency expanded steadily, enhanced by the country's need for strong leadership during the Great Depression, World War II, and the cold war. The men who occupied the office of President came to exercise a degree of authority—especially in foreign affairs and warmaking—denied to earlier Presidents. Congress had acquiesced in this exercise of authority by the Presidents because it did not want to appear devisive in times that called for national unity. An occasional protest was made by individual senators or representatives about the excesses of the imperial Presidents, but Congress made no concerted effort to limit their power. The result was a steady erosion of the part Congress should play in the federal government under the Constitution.

The new Congress of the 1970s, however, began to alter this

pattern of acquiescence. The House and Senate strengthened their resources in order to deal on a par with the executive branch and in several instances challenged the power of the President directly. A reform of the budget-making process gave Congress the ability to handle complex financial affairs and to create its own programs for revenue and expenditure in a way never before possible. Important presidential appointments to the Supreme Court were considered and rejected—a way of telling the President that Congress, too, had the power to approve appointments. In foreign affairs, the new Congress restricted presidential authority in several areas, but most important in the area of war. And, finally, the new Congress confronted the President directly through investigation of his activities and behavior and concluded that he was guilty of impeachable offenses.

I

FOR MANY years, the need for a change in the way Congress considered the federal budget was painfully obvious. Congress had no centralized budget authority and no experts capable of understanding and overseeing the development of the budget as a whole. By contrast, the executive branch had the Bureau of the Budget (now the Office of Management and Budget), which was well staffed by economic professionals experienced in the complexities of federal revenues and spending. Each year when the Congress considered the budget handed down by the President, it divided the budget into many small parts to be distributed among various committees and subcommittees for deliberation. Each committee or subcommittee then worked on its small part with little or no awareness of what the rest of Congress was doing. As a result, few members of Congress understood the whole picture, and no one had complete control of the final budget that would emerge.

The lack of congressional control of the budget played into the President's hands. Because his staff possessed the information and expertise necessary to plan the budget, he could make his own programs and policies felt more directly than Congress could. A President strong on defense, for instance, could increase defense spending, whereas a President with a large number of social programs on his legislative agenda could emphasize these programs. Congress could pick away at these programs and decrease or increase the money available for them, but it could not deny the fact that the President had the initiative when it came to the federal budget.

In addition to being able to match the executive branch's budget expertise, there were several other reasons for budget reform. Many members of Congress had long expressed a desire to be able to exert more control over the appropriations process in order to place some limit on the rapid growth in government spending and the yearly rise in the national deficit. Especially troublesome to them was the seventy-five percent of the budget that many experts regarded as "relatively uncontrollable under existing law," such as social security, welfare, government contracts that required future funding, and debts already acquired through basic legislation, such as the need to pay the interest on the national debt.

More liberal-minded members of Congress advocated budget reform because of the need they saw for greater fiscal planning and greater control by the House and Senate of national priorities. Better control of fiscal policy meant that Congress would be able to provide the right sort of economic stimulus or restraint, in order to help a weak economy or encourage one that showed signs of health. The power to establish spending priorities would enable the House and Senate to establish their own programs for the nation rather than rely on the budget priorities of the President.

The Legislative Reorganization Act of 1946 had tried to come to terms with budgetary problems, but had failed. The act provided that Congress establish the amount of money to be appropriated for each fiscal year. The ceiling was to be decided by a Joint Budget Committee composed of all the members of the House and Senate Appropriations Committees, the House Ways and Means Committee, and the Senate Finance Committee—a total of one hundred members. Over the next three years, the joint committee, whose enormous size made it unwieldy, disagreed on basic matters and by 1949 had failed to produce a legislative budget.

In 1950, Congress tried another approach. An "omnibus bill" plan was adopted in which the numerous appropriations proposals were combined in one bill. The omnibus bill plan was at first successful and resulted in several benefits. It took less time for Congress to consider the budget, and the final budget decided upon spent less federal money than the budget submitted by the President—the two goals sought by budget reformers. But in 1951, the omnibus bill plan was scrapped because of the opposition of powerful committee chairmen who feared that the plan deprived them of the right to review important sections of the budget.

Several other plans were discussed in the following years, but none was ever made into law. It was not until 1972, when Congress established a Joint Study Committee on Budget Control, that serious consideration of budget reform was once again in the air. The joint committee was largely the result of congressional opposition to the use of impoundment by President Nixon.

Nixon advanced the use of impoundment, by which he refused to spend money already allocated by Congress, for what he and many others regarded as good reasons. It was his way of holding spending down and challenging what he called the "fiscal irresponsibility" of Congress. As we saw in the fifth chapter, however, the problem with impoundment was not in its aims, but in its methods.

Under the Constitution, the President simply did not have the power to impound funds in the manner Nixon used. Spending was finally the right of Congress, and it was this right the Joint Study Committee on Budget Control sought to guarantee.

The joint committee issued a report with recommendations for reform that was finally adopted, after intense debate, as the Budget Act of 1974. The act contained two wide-ranging proposals for budget committees and a budget timetable, and it directly attacked the problem of presidential impoundment of expenditures.

Budget committees. Budget committees were established in both the House of Representatives and the Senate. Both committees were required to report at least two budget resolutions each year, investigate the impact of existing and proposed legislative programs on the budget, and oversee the operations of the Congressional Budget Office. The House committee was to have twenty-five members, who were restricted to a maximum of four years' service on the committee in each ten-year period. Of the twenty-five members, five came from Appropriations, five from Ways and Means, and two from the leadership of each political party. The Senate committee was given sixteen members, with no limitation on tenure and with a membership chosen like that of any other Senate committee.

Each committee was also supplied with a staff to aid it in its activities. The House Budget Committee was given forty professionals and twenty-five clerical workers, the Senate fifty-five professionals and thirty clericals. The professional staff members have budgetary and financial expertise most members of Congress do not have and supply the detailed analyses of revenue and spending that committee resolutions are based upon.

But the major portion of information and analysis was to be provided by the Congressional Budget Office (CBO). The CBO must monitor the economy and estimate its impact on the budget, improve the flow and quality of information available to the

House and Senate on the budget, and perform the difficult task of estimating the costs of alternative budget choices and priorities. The CBO has on hand computers and other modern electronic equipment to help it in its work.

Budget timetable. One of the most extraordinary innovations of the Budget Act was to establish a precise timetable for the consideration and submission of budget material throughout the fiscal year. The exact details of this timetable need not concern us here, except to say that the timetable was adopted so that Congress would have a schedule to follow that would allow time for careful consideration and review of the budget from top to bottom.

As the fiscal year progresses, the timetable sets deadlines for the completion of different stages of the budgetary process until a final bill, reconciling the positions of the House and Senate, is adopted. For instance, all advice and data from the congressional committees are to be received by the budget committees by March 15 of each year. On April 1, the CBO reports its findings to the budget committees, and so on, until the budget is completed on September 25 for the new fiscal year, which now begins on October 1.

The precise timetable was adopted in order to solve the problems that had given rise to the need for budget reform. The timetable, for instance, allows Congress to set targets and ceilings, it permits careful study of budget alternatives so that priorities can be established, and it allows Congress to come to terms with the need for economic stimulus or restraint, depending, of course, on the state of the economy. In the haphazard revenue and appropriations system that existed before the Budget Act was passed, Congress did not have the time or ability to handle these problems successfully. But now, due to the timetable that outlines the problems to be attacked and provides a framework for activity, Congress can deal with budget problems more effectively.

The precise timetable and the greater amount of economic expertise and information available to Congress have helped the House and Senate to meet the experts of the executive branch on an equal basis. Gone are the days when the President's priorities and policies seemed to dominate the budget-making process. The Congress can now make its own priorities and policies felt and can add its own creative and innovative approaches on the budget to those of the President.

Moreover, the Budget Act of 1974 required that Congress have a say in all presidential impoundments of federal funds. The Act divided all impoundments into two categories, deferrals and recisions. A deferral occurs when the President merely delays or postpones the spending of appropriated funds. If a President chooses to defer, however, he can do so only until the end of the current fiscal year and he can defer only on the grounds that the funds need not be spent in order to achieve the original intent of Congress in appropriating the funds. If a majority of either the House or the Senate requires, he must stop his impoundment by deferral and spend the allocated funds.

A recision action means that the President has decided not to spend the appropriated funds at all. In this case, he must submit a recision bill to Congress, and this bill must win majorities in both houses within forty-five days in order to become law. If the House and Senate fail to pass the recision bill, then the President must spend the money. If the President refuses to comply with a congressional resolution overruling an impoundment, the comptroller general is instructed to go to court to get an order requiring the compliance of the President.

II

IN ADDITION to budgetary reform, the new Congress tackled the problem of executive secrecy. The elaborate system of secrecy that led to the classification of documents as "top secret" and sought to keep them from Congress and public alike is largely an invention of the twentieth century. It began to appear during World War I and grew by leaps and bounds during World War II and the cold war. The need for secrecy was based on the notion of "national security" and the belief that information that leaked from the executive branch could strengthen the power of the enemy.

There are, no doubt, several legitimate areas in which secrecy is of great importance. These include sensitive negotiations with foreign nations where openness might harm the negotiating process and intelligence activities where the revelation of what has been learned might close down valuable sources of information in the future. In addition, personal dossiers maintained by the government should be kept privileged to protect an individual's right to privacy.

But the secrecy system that began to develop in World War II and grew during the years of the cold war encompassed far more areas than these. In the words of historian Arthur Schlesinger, Jr., the secrecy system surpassed its original and defensible goals to become "an extravagant and indefensible system of denial" of information to Congress, to the press, and to the American people.

The growth of secrecy was all the more questionable because it had no basis in law. It was fed by the belief that in serious matters only the President should know the facts and only he could act quickly and forcefully to protect the nation. The denial of information to Congress, however, was contrary to the purposes of the Constitution and to the intentions of the Founding Fathers. James Madison had declared that "a popular government without popular information or the means of acquiring it, is but a prologue to a farce or a tragedy; or, perhaps both." It was Madison's belief that "knowledge will forever govern ignorance; and a people who mean to be their own governors must arm themselves with the power which knowledge gives."

As early as the 1950s, there were members of Congress who questioned the need for the elaborate system of secrecy. In 1951, for instance, conservative Senator Robert Taft warned that "the result of the general practice of secrecy . . . has been to deprive the Senate and Congress of the substance of the powers conferred on them by the Constitution." A few years later, Senator Thomas Hennings (Democrat, Missouri), chairman of the Constitutional Rights Subcommittee of the Senate, and Representative John Moss (Democrat, New York), chairman of the Government Information Subcommittee of the House, uncovered piece after piece of "top secret" material that had no business being classified. Another opponent of excessive government secrecy, Vice-President Richard Nixon, said that in his opinion "the whole concept of a return to secrecy in peacetime demonstrates a profound misunderstanding of the role of a free press. . . . The plea for security could well become a cloak for errors, misjudgments, and other failings of government."

Nixon's statement, made in 1961, was indeed true, but it did not express the opinions of the majority of Congress or of the American people. The general feeling was that communism was a dangerous threat that called for extraordinary action, even if that action meant the destruction of the constitutional right of information. By the 1970s, the secrecy system in the Departments of Defense and State, the Atomic Energy Commission, and the National Aeronautics and Space Administration was costing the taxpayer more than $60 million a year. William Florence, a former Pentagon security officer, testified before Congress that there were twenty million documents in the defense security system alone and that "less than one-half of one percent . . . actually contain information qualifying for even the lowest defense classification."

In other words, the secrecy system had become far more than a method to preserve national security. It now functioned as a means to assure the primacy of the executive branch and to cloak its activities in a mantle of mystery. Because the chief executive was the man who controlled the "facts" and had access to the "top secrets," he could increase his own power, manipulate the public and the Congress, and disguise his own mistakes.

The first effective questioning by Congress of the practice of executive secrecy came in 1969 and 1970. Suspicious of secret commitments abroad that had been made by the President, the Senate established the Foreign Relations Subcommittee on United States Security Agreements and Commitments Abroad. The committee sent a two-man team on a fact-finding mission to twenty-five countries. Further investigations followed, including detailed, closed-door hearings that uncovered a number of previously unknown commitments to foreign nations. These commitments, it was feared could embroil the United States in war, yet few of them had been duly considered by the Congress, and few were known to the American people.

But the issue of government secrecy was brought to a dramatic head in 1971 with the publication of the so-called Pentagon papers. Daniel Ellsberg, a former employee of the executive branch, had assembled a group of highly classified documents bearing on the way the government waged the Vietnam War. He turned them over to the *New York Times*, which proceeded to publish them (they also appeared in the *Washington Post*) in June. In the Senate, Senator Mike Gravel (Democrat, Alaska) read the documents before the Senate Subcommittee on Buildings and Grounds, from whence they made their way into the Congressional Record.

President Nixon, now reversing his earlier position on executive secrecy, believed that the publication of the papers would do "immediate and irreparable" damage to the government and sought to stop their publication. His administration brought a suit against the *Times* and the *Post* based on the Official Secrets Act. The issue went to the Supreme Court, which decided six to three in favor of the newspapers. The Pentagon papers were published. Many observers believed that if the information in them had been available to Congress six years earlier when it passed the Gulf of Tonkin resolution, which gave congressional approval to the Vietnam War, the resolution would never have succeeded. It was an example of the practice of executive secrecy misleading the Congress and causing it to act outside of its own best interests.

In 1972, the year after the controversy over the Pentagon papers, the Senate established a special ten-member Committee to Study Questions Related to Secret and Confidential Government Documents, co-chaired by the majority and minority leaders. In its report, published the next year, the committee maintained that Congress should take a close look at the power it had given the President to classify government documents and keep them out of the reach of Congress; the secrecy system, it implied, had all too frequently been used to upset the balance of power between Congress and the President in favor of the chief executive.

Similar investigations in the 1970s looked into the secret activities of the CIA and the FBI. These investigations uncovered many abuses of law by the two agencies and frequent violations of the rules and statutes that Congress had established to govern their activities. The Senate Select Intelligence Committee, for instance, found that Republican and Democratic administrations since World War II had used the FBI for secret surveillance of a number of people and political organizations. The committee also learned that the CIA, which by law was supposed to confine its activities to other countries and not work within American borders, had been active in internal affairs in the United States. The discoveries suggested that the two agencies, which had been established to meet legitimate national needs, had been used to an extent by the executive branch to further its own partisan interests. The investigations led to new laws that placed limits on the power of the FBI and CIA to violate the constitutional rights of American citizens.

III

BETWEEN THE administrations of Franklin Roosevelt and Richard Nixon, as we saw in Chapter Five, the executive branch expanded its authority in foreign policy and decisions concerning war. Indeed, it was in these areas that the imperial presidency took deepest root and interfered most widely in powers traditionally granted to Congress. The source of expanded presidential authority in foreign affairs and war was the belief, fed by the American participation in World War II and by the cold war, that the United States was "the guardian of the free world." In support of this ideal, most Americans thought that it was necessary to concentrate power in the President. Only the President could fully understand what commitments had to be made abroad to preserve American interests, and only he could deploy the armed services swiftly in time of need.

In the 1950s, Congress had considered a means to limit the power of the President in foreign affairs. Senator John Bricker (Republican, Ohio), a conservative, believed that the expansion of American commitments abroad would inevitably lead to policies that violated state and federal laws and the Constitution. In 1953 and again in 1954 and 1956, he proposed the so-called Bricker amendment, which required all treaties to become effective "only through the enactment of appropriate legislation by the Congress." The Bricker amendment also placed limitations on executive agreements with foreign nations and gave Congress greater power over such agreements. The Bricker amendment, however, failed to pass Congress, even though there was significant support for it.

During the Vietnam War, congressional interest in restricting the foreign policy and war-making powers of the President revived. Step by step, Congress challenged the authority of the President, culminating in the War Powers Act of 1973.

• In 1970, Senator Clifford Case (Republican, New Jersey) sponsored a bill that required the Secretary of State to submit to Congress the final text of any international agreement made by the executive branch within sixty days of its completion. The Case bill met the problem of national security by requiring that any agreement involving national security be submitted on a classified basis to the House and Senate Foreign Affairs Committees. The Nixon administration opposed the bill, but it passed anyway.

• In 1970, Congress repealed the Tonkin Gulf Resolution of 1964, which it had formerly passed overwhelmingly. President Nixon ignored the repeal, even though it expressed the growing congressional opposition to the war.

• In the same year, after President Nixon ordered the invasion of Cambodia, Senators John Sherman Cooper (Republican, Kentucky) and Frank Church made a proposal that would bar the use of federal funds to finance the invasion. Later a watered-down bill passed the Senate; this bill barred the use of American ground troops in Cambodia, but it did not bar the use of aircraft.

• In 1971, the Senate adopted proposals by Majority Leader Mike Mansfield that called for the withdrawal of troops from Vietnam by a certain deadline.

• In 1972, the Senate adopted by roll-call vote a bill that called for cutting off funds for American participation in the Vietnam War within four months of the passage of the bill. The House, however, refused to accept these stipulations.

• When the United States pulled out of Vietnam after the peace agreement of January 27, 1973, but continued to bomb Laos and Cambodia, the House and Senate passed bills requiring the cutoff of funds for all military operations in Indochina. The bill stopped the use of all appropriations for the direct or indirect financing of all combat activities.

• Later in 1973, the War Powers Act was passed by a two-thirds vote of the House and Senate after it had been vetoed by President Nixon. Supported by Senator Jacob Javits (Republican, New York), it was the first bill in American history to define and attempt to limit presidential war-making authority. Javits defended the bill by saying, "After two hundred years, at last something will have been done about codifying the implementation of the most awesome power in the possession of any sovereignty and giving the broad representation of the people in Congress a voice in it." This is important, he concluded, because "we have just learned the hard lesson that wars cannot be successfully fought except with the consent of the people and with their support."

The War Powers Act contained, among others, the following provisions. It specifically granted power to the President to commit American armed forces to hostilities or to places where hostilities were imminent, but only after a declaration of war, a statutory authorization, or a national emergency created by an attack upon the United States, its territories, possessions, or armed forces. In addition, the act urged the President to consult with the Congress "in every possible instance" before he committed forces into conflict.

The President was required to submit a report in writing within forty-eight hours to the Speaker of the House and the president pro tempore of the Senate of any commitment or substantial enlargement of combat forces abroad, except in cases related to supply, replacement, repair, or training of those forces. Supplementary reports were required every six months while the forces were engaged. The Speaker and the president pro tempore were authorized to call Congress into session, if it was absent from Washington, to consider the President's reports. Congress had the power to terminate the commitment of forces, if both houses agreed to order the President to disengage the troops.

Many critics of the War Powers Act believed that it had given the President too much authority because it granted him the written power to respond to emergencies by employing the armed services. The President could now activate American troops, they argued, and commit them to hostilities in the certain knowledge that public opinion would support his action and that Congress, in the heat of the moment, would have to agree to his action. Others, however, believed that the War Powers Act offered the best possible means to limit the power of the President and assure that the United States never again became involved in conflicts like the Vietnam War.

The War Powers Act was followed by other congressional efforts to assert its authority in the areas of foreign policy and war. In 1975, Congress imposed a ban on the shipment of arms to Turkey, a NATO ally, in spite of presidential opposition to the ban. President Ford urged Congress to reconsider its move, but the ban had been only partially lifted by the end of the year. Similarly the Senate blocked funds earmarked for two of the three guerrilla armies fighting in the African nation of Angola. The Senate feared that an American commitment to Angola would involve the United States in a Vietnam-like war.

IV

THE CONSTITUTION grants to the President the right to appoint judges to the Supreme Court with the "advice and consent" of the Senate. In most cases, the Senate has chosen to accept presidential appointments to the high court after an investigation of the nominee's background and qualifications. On rare occasions, however, it has chosen to exercise its authority of advice and consent by rejecting the President's choice. One of the most striking challenges to the imperial presidency made by Congress was the rejection of two Nixon appointees in a row. Not since 1894, during the second administration of Grover Cleveland had the Senate dealt a President a similar blow.

President Nixon's first appointment to the Supreme Court, Warren Burger, was passed with no trouble. The Senate quickly voted to confirm him by a vote of seventy-four to three to replace Chief Justice Earl Warren, who was retiring. But in May, 1969, Nixon was offered a second opportunity to name a person to the court when Justice Abe Fortas resigned after he had been accused of accepting a fee from the family foundation of a convicted stock manipulator.

Nixon chose as his nominee Clement Haynsworth, Jr., of South Carolina, the chief judge of the Fourth Circuit Court of Appeals. Haynsworth, the President said, shared his own conservative interpretation of the Constitution and American law. Haynsworth, however, met opposition from the beginning. Civil rights groups and labor leaders found him unacceptable because his judicial decisions, they said, had frequently been anti-civil rights and anti-labor.

In the Senate, opposition to Haynsworth centered on conflict of interest. Many senators were convinced that he had been insensitive to the appearance of ethical impropriety by participating in cases in which his personal financial interests were involved. In such cases, it is customary for judges to excuse themselves and not participate in a verdict. But by remaining on the cases, Haynsworth had opened himself to charges that he had personally benefited from his position as a judge.

The Senate Judiciary Committee, which must approve all nominations to the Supreme Court before they are sent to the full Senate, accepted Haynsworth by a vote of ten to seven. The majority opinion described him as "extraordinarily well qualified" and declared that the objections raised against his appointment were without substance.

On the Senate floor, however, the Haynsworth opposition was led by Senator Birch Bayh (Democrat, Indiana). Bayh rallied many of his colleagues around him. From the White House, the Nixon administration exerted pressure for Haynsworth's acceptance. But when a roll-call vote on the nomination came up, more than three months after the President had named Haynsworth to the Court, he was rejected forty-five to fifty-five. The defeat would not have been possible without the support of seventeen Republicans, including three Republican Senate leaders, who joined thirty-eight Democrats in a *no* vote.

Early the next year, Nixon sent a second nomination to the Senate for consideration. G. Harrold Carswell, the new nominee, was a judge in the Fifth Circuit Court of Appeals and a resident of Florida. Like Haynsworth, Carswell was a southerner with a reputation for judicial conservatism and a strict constructionist when it came to constitutional law.

Most senators did not want a repeat of the bitter struggle that led to the defeat of Haynsworth and at first looked with favor on Carswell. But soon it became clear that Carswell was a man of mediocre abilities, competent, perhaps, for his present position on the circuit court, but unlikely material for the Supreme Court. In addition, investigation uncovered the fact that Carswell in 1948 had publicly pledged himself to the principle of white supremacy. For most senators, it was unthinkable that a man capable of blatant racism could sit on the high court. Carswell claimed that he had changed his opinion since 1948 and that he no longer believed in the natural superiority of the white race. But his membership in an all-white private club that rejected blacks and others, seemed to undermine his claims that he had changed his opinions.

Carswell received approval from the Judiciary Committee, by a vote of thirteen to four. His nomination seemed likely to pass the Senate. But when it moved to the Senate floor, his opponents succeeded in postponing a vote until after the traditional Easter recess of Congress. This gave them time to lobby and apply pressure to those who were uncertain about their final votes. When the Senate returned, the outcome was no longer certain. Most observers believed that the sides were now evenly drawn, with roughly the same number of senators opposed as were prepared to accept the nomination.

At about this time, President Nixon wrote a letter to Senator William Saxbe (Republican, Ohio). In the letter, he mentioned that he, as President, was "the one person entrusted by the Constitution with the power of appointment." He agreed that the Senate had the power of advice and consent but seemed to imply that this power was a mere formality. "But if the Senate attempts to substitute its judgment as to who should be appointed," he concluded, "the traditional constitutional balance is in jeopardy and the duty of the President under the Constitution is impaired."

This was not an opinion shared by the Senate. The first vote on the nomination of Carswell came on April 6 as a vote on a motion to recommit the nomination for consideration by the Judiciary Committee. Opponents hoped that by returning the nomination to the committee, they could bury it. But the recommittal effort was defeated by a vote of forty-four to fifty-two. The Nixon administration had won the first round.

The recommittal vote was followed by two days of lobbying with a final vote taken on April 8. Carswell lost his chance to serve on the Supreme Court by a vote of forty-four to fifty-one. Once again, Republicans who had defected from the position of the administration were responsible for the outcome. Thirteen of their number had joined thirty-eight Democrats in the vote against the nomination.

Nixon's third nomination for the seat vacated by Abe Fortas was readily accepted by a vote of ninety-four to zero. But the

President never overcame his disappointment at the rejection of Haynsworth and Carswell. To him and his supporters, rejection seemed politically motivated, the judgment of a Democratic Senate against a Republican President. From the Senate's point of view, however, the rejections seemed perfectly justified and in keeping with the Senate's right to refuse to accept nominations it considers unworthy. To the senators who voted against the nominations, it seemed obvious that a *no* vote was required if the Senate was to maintain its integrity. After all, both nominees had been found wanting in very serious matters, and to approve them simply because the President had appointed them would have been to forsake the Senate's duty under the Constitution.

The new congressional budget system, the attack on executive secrecy, the redefinition of the role of Congress in foreign policy and war-making decisions, and the rejection of two presidential nominations to the Supreme Court were all part of an attempt to restore the legislative branch to its rightful place in the American government. The new budget system and the attack on secrecy gave Congress new expertise and new sources of information once available only to the executive branch. The redefinition of congressional powers in foreign policy and war-making and the rejection of the Supreme Court nominees showed that the new Congress could challenge the imperial presidency and make its influence felt on important issues. Congress now seemed well on the way toward playing a part equal to the President's, as the framers of the Constitution had envisioned.

CHAPTER NINE

CONGRESS AND THE WATERGATE AFFAIR

If Government becomes a lawbreaker, it breeds contempt for the law; it invites every man to become a law unto himself; it invites anarchy—Louis D. Brandeis, Associate Justice of the Supreme Court

I

THE WATERGATE affair grew from small beginnings. On the night of June 16–17, 1972, six men were discovered inside the Democratic national headquarters in the Watergate, an expensive hotel and apartment complex in Washington, D.C. Exactly what the burglars hoped to accomplish still remains a mystery. The Democratic headquarters contained little information of any significance that they could steal, nor would they be able to learn much by bugging its telephones. Even more mysterious was the fact that the burglars carried personal identification, as well as cash in the form of $100 bills, which would be traced, by later investigation, to the Republican party's Committee to Reelect the President.

In September, the six men were indicted by a Washington grand jury along with two of their bosses, Howard Hunt and Gordon

Liddy, who were known to have held low-echelon positions at the White House. Their trial was set for January, 1973, two months after the presidential elections in November. The case might have died at this point had it not been for the curiosity of two young reporters for the *Washington Post*, Bob Woodward and Carl Bernstein. Woodward and Bernstein began to ask questions and seek answers. What were the burglars doing at the Watergate? Did their orders come only from Hunt and Liddy or had they come from higher up? Had advisers close to the President been involved? Had the President himself been involved? The answers they found to these questions over the next several months broke the Watergate affair wide open and ultimately led to the resignation of President Nixon.

II

Congressional investigation of the Watergate affair began slowly. In August, 1972, the General Accounting Office (GAO), an agency of Congress, uncovered significant violations of the Campaign Finance Act of 1971 by Nixon's reelection finance committee. In October, Wright Patman, chairman of the House Banking and Currency Committee, attempted to get his committee to agree to an investigation of Republican campaign financing that would have included subpoenaing forty individuals and organizations. Still uncertain about the Watergate affair, however, the committee rejected the proposal, twenty to fifteen.

The Senate proved less reluctant to act. Majority Leader Mike Mansfield began to put the gears in motion in November, 1972, by urging Senator James Eastland (Democrat, Mississippi), who headed the Judiciary Committee, to agree to an investigation that would be conducted by Sam Ervin, head of the Judiciary Subcommittee on Constitutional Rights. Mansfield wrote a letter to

Eastland that said, "The Watergate incident contains implications of great gravity for all political activity in the nation." What may be involved, Mansfield concluded, "is not only a question of federal crimes which are, properly, subject to juridical disposition but also a cynical and dangerous intrusion into the integrity of the electoral processes by which the people of the nation choose the trustees of federal office."

To Ervin, Mansfield wrote another letter on the same day. "I suggest that you and Senator Eastland," he said, "discuss this matter and make a recommendation to the Senate for a single instrument of investigation. It seems to me imperative to concentrate the energy and resources of the Senate on an inquiry into the substance of the Watergate affair." That affair, he added, "has raised the very fundamental question of the right of every American to assurance from government of the integrity of the Federal electoral process. . . . In truth, the question is not political; it is Constitutional. At stake is the continued vitality of the electoral process in the governmental structure of the nation."

On February 7, 1973, the Senate voted seventy-seven to zero to establish a select committee that would "conduct an investigation and study the extent, if any, to which illegal, improper, or unethical activities were engaged in by any persons . . . in the presidential election of 1972." The select committee was given the power to subpoena any persons "who the select committee believes have knowledge or information" about such activities. As a result of its investigation, the select committee was to report to the Senate any recommendations it might have for legislation "necessary . . . to safeguard the electoral process by which the President of the United States is chosen." Among the Senators who served on the committee in addition to Ervin were Howard Baker (Republican, Tennessee), Herman Talmadge (Democrat, Georgia), Lowell Weicker (Republican, Connecticut), Daniel

Inouye (Democrat, Hawaii), Joseph Montoya (Democrat, New Mexico), and Edward Gurney (Republican, Florida).

As chief counsel and staff director for the committee, Ervin hired an expert on the legalities of wiretapping, Samuel Dash, who headed the Institute for Criminal Law and Procedure at Georgetown University. The committee was well staffed, with twenty-five lawyers, twenty investigators, eight consultants, six administrators, fifty-one secretaries and clerical workers, twenty-two specialized research assistants, twenty-two computer experts, and three volunteers. The computer experts manned the committee's computer, which helped to organize the enormous amount of testimony collected over the next few months. Few select committees have been so well prepared for the work they were to perform. Indeed, some Washington observers noted the disparity between the committee's staff and resources and the small number of lawyers and assistants the President assembled to support his cause. It was a turnabout from the days when a well-prepared executive branch, backed by experts and information, faced a Congress that had few resources in staff and expertise.

The hearings, which were carried by public television, began on May 17, 1973. During the first weeks, the list of witnesses who testified before the committee was impressive and included everyone from James McCord, one of the men caught in the Watergate, and John Dean, the President's former counsel, to Nixon's most intimate advisers, Robert Haldeman and John Ehrlichman. Jeb Magruder, who had worked for the Committee to Reelect the President, was the first witness to give testimony damaging to the White House when he admitted that his orders to burglarize the Democratic headquarters had come from John Mitchell, the former attorney general of the United States and a close friend of the President. Ten days later, John Dean implicated the President himself in an illegal conspiracy to cover up

White House involvement in Watergate. Dean gave the select committee some fifty documents pertinent to the investigation.

For the press and the American public, the most unexpected revelation came during the testimony of Alexander Butterfield, a former White House aide who had become head of the Federal Aviation Administration. Butterfield told the committee of the existence of a voice-activated taping system in the Oval Office that recorded the President's conversations. His testimony was significant because it meant that Dean's allegation that the President had participated in an illegal cover-up could now be proved or disproved. The committee subpoenaed the President, asking for the tapes of five particular conversations as well as for several other relevant documents.

When John Ehrlichman, Nixon's former chief domestic adviser appeared before the committee, he defended the activities of the President by declaring that any President had the inherent power, in the name of national security, to commit acts that would be illegal if committed by the average citizen. Sam Ervin disagreed. "I do not believe," Ervin said, "the President has any power at all except such as the Constitution expressly gives him or such as are necessarily inferred from the expression of those powers. I think the Constitution was written that way to keep the President, and, of course, the Congress, from exercising tyrannical power."

Later that same day, Ervin eloquently summed up what he believed to be the chief crime of the Watergate affair. Citing English common law, which forms the basis of American law, Ervin reminded his listeners that a break-in constituted a basic violation of an individual's rights. "The poorest man in his cottage may bid defiance to all the forces of the crown," Ervin said. His house "may be frail, its roof may shake, the wind may blow through it, the storm may enter, the rain may enter, but the king of England cannot enter. All his force dares not cross the threshold of the ruined tenement." But yet, Ervin concluded, "we are told here today . . . that what the king of England cannot do, the President of the United States can." Ervin's statement was one of the high points of the hearings. It succinctly affirmed the committee's belief that no one was above the law, not even the President, and that when a President violated the nation's laws, he could be challenged for his actions and held responsible for them.

III

FROM THE beginning of the hearings, the Ervin committee struggled with the President to obtain information and testimony. Nixon at first claimed executive privilege in all matters pertaining to the case and refused to allow any of his aides to appear as witnesses. By April, 1973, however, he had reversed himself. White House employees and other government officials, he said, "are expected fully to cooperate in this matter. I condemn any attempts to cover up in this case, no matter who is involved."

But in May, Nixon changed his position once again and claimed executive privilege in matters that pertained directly to the President or national security. He also stated that he personally refused to give written or oral testimony before the committee, because for the President to do so would be "constitutionally inappropriate." In a letter to Sam Ervin, Nixon gave more specific reasons for his refusal to testify or turn over personal documents. "Formulation of sound public policy," he wrote, "requires that the President and his personal staff be able to communicate among themselves in complete candor. . . . If I were to testify before the committee, irreparable damage would be done to the constitutional principle of separation of powers."

The situation was now a standoff: the rights of the President to privacy balanced by the rights of the Senate for information.

It was Butterfield's revelation about the White House tapes that helped to break the logjam. The Ervin committee requested five recordings from the President and, when he refused to comply with the request, took the issue to the courts. On August 29, 1973, Judge John J. Sirica of the United States District Court in Washington ruled that the President should turn the tapes over to him for review. The President protested, but in October, the court of appeals sustained Sirica's request to review the tapes. A majority of judges on the appeals court ruled that executive privilege was a "qualified" privilege that always had to be weighed against the public's right to information. But later in the same month, Judge Sirica came to the conclusion that he had no jurisdiction in the case and did not have the authority to turn the tapes over to the Senate committee.

It was a major blow to the select committee, which had hoped it would receive the information it needed. Congress now passed a bill specifically granting Judge Sirica the jurisdiction in the case that he had claimed not to have. Once again, the committee requested the five tapes. When the request went to the courts this time, Sirica disqualified himself and the case was heard by District Court Judge Gerhard Gesell. Gesell ruled that the President, under law, had to respond to the demand for the tapes because the Senate committee had been specific and particular in its demands. Nixon, Gesell added, must provide a detailed statement that explained which parts of the subpoenaed tapes he considered to be covered by executive privilege and this statement "must be signed by the President, for only he can invoke the privilege at issue."

Once again, Nixon refused to turn over the tapes because to do so would "not be in the public interest." Gesell allowed the President to keep the tapes, but for a different reason. To turn over the tapes to the Senate committee, he argued, would make it difficult to obtain an unbiased jury for the trials that had arisen from the Watergate affair. Gesell had not supported the notion of executive privilege; he had moved merely to protect the trial rights of those like John Dean, Jeb Magruder, and others involved in the case, most of whom would later go to jail. Nixon did not have to submit the tapes to the Ervin committee, but the question of whether or not he would later have to submit them to a federal court was still up in the air.

In February, 1974, the Senate Watergate committee agreed to terminate its public hearings. Most of its work was completed. In the long run, its failure to obtain the tapes it sought was unimportant, for the committee had uncovered much that had given the public a picture of what had been involved in Watergate. The committee had discovered the existence of the tapes, which proved to be the key to the whole case, and it had revealed the whole range of "dirty tricks" and illegal acts committed during the 1972 presidential campaign. Etched forever on the minds of the people who watched the Senate Watergate hearings on television were the confessions of Nixon's loyal assistants who had approved wiretappings, burglaries, and other acts all in the name of the man they wanted to see reelected President.

IV

THE RESPONSIBILITY for the remainder of the Watergate affair fell on the shoulders of the special prosecutor, the courts, and the House of Representatives. Soon after the affair began to gain wide public attention, Nixon appointed a Harvard professor of law, Archibald Cox, to be special prosecutor. The special prosecutor, although an appointee of the chief executive, was to conduct an impartial and complete investigation in the Watergate matter and render a verdict. Nixon hoped that his decision to appoint Cox, a widely respected man, would help to quiet the demands of those who were clamoring to know exactly what had happened at the Watergate.

Cox proceeded to conduct his investigation, but when he requested that Nixon turn over the White House tapes to the special prosecutor's staff, the President fired him. On the same day, October 20, 1973, Nixon accepted the resignation of his attorney general, Elliot Richardson, and then fired the deputy attorney general, William Ruckelshaus, after both men had refused to carry out the presidential order to fire the special prosecutor. The removal of the three prominent men was labeled the "Saturday Night Massacre" by the press. To replace Cox, Nixon chose Leon Jaworski of Texas. If the President hoped that his firing of Cox would still the requests for the tapes, he was mistaken. Jaworski too subpoenaed the President for the recordings, and when the President denied him access to them, Jaworski took the case all the way to the Supreme Court.

The Saturday Night Massacre also started another movement the President had not anticipated. On the Monday following the massacre, the House of Representatives saw a number of impeachment resolutions introduced. Pressure for an investigation of the President's activities grew over the next few months, and on February 6, 1974, the House voted 410 to 4 to conduct an inquiry. It charged the House Judiciary Committee "to investigate fully and completely whether sufficient grounds exist for the House of Representatives to exercise its constitutional power to impeach Richard M. Nixon, President of the United States of America."

Peter Rodino (Democrat, New Jersey), a moderate, was chairman of the Judiciary Committee. On the committee were thirty-eight men and women—twenty-one Democrats and seventeen Republicans. They represented a wide variety of constituencies and differed markedly in political opinion. Liberal Paul Sarbanes (Democrat, Maryland), a former Rhodes scholar, was an outspoken Nixon opponent. Charles Wiggins (Republican, California), on the other hand, was a conservative and a strong defender of the President. Other members included Barbara Jordan (Democrat, Texas), a black, who gained nationwide fame for her careful articulation of the legal questions at hand, William Cohen (Republican, Maine), a young moderate, Tom Railsback (Republican, Illinois), and Elizabeth Holtzman (Democrat, New York).

Rodino settled on John Doar as chief counsel for the committee. Doar's reputation had been made in the early 1960s as an employee of the Justice Department under President Kennedy, when he had led many of the struggles in the South to bring equality to blacks. He was known for his courage and incorruptibility, but most important, Rodino saw in him a man who would stand firm when faced with the difficult task of challenging the President. "My task," Doar said, "was to make the Constitution work, to make the process of impeachment work—whether to a trial or to a vindication didn't matter."

Doar's basic requirement for the staff he chose to work with him was that they had not expressed an opinion on Richard Nixon one way or the other. He wanted to obtain the facts and not run a "witch hunt" directed solely at undermining the President. The staff collected data from every available source—from the Senate Watergate Committee, from newspapers, and from the White House. In the end, the data would fill forty volumes and would be used by the members of the Judiciary Committee in arriving at an impeachment verdict.

The members of the Judiciary Committee had their own difficult work to perform. There was little precedent to work on. The impeachment of Andrew Johnson more than one hundred years earlier was dissimilar to Nixon's case in many ways. The Constitution said that the President could be impeached for "treason, bribery, or other high crimes and misdemeanors." It was clear that Nixon was not guilty of treason or of bribery. But what were "other high crimes and misdemeanors"? It was necessary that the committee be precise in any accusations it brought against the President. Any vagueness, ambiguity, or uncertainty would reflect on the committee and lead to the charge that it had attacked the President out of political motives and not for serious reasons of constitutional law. The committee members were mindful too that the work they did and the way in which they performed their task would serve as a model for any later impeachment proceedings that might arise in years to come.

The notion of impeachment was derived from English common law and parliamentary practice. The word itself came from an old French word that meant "to stop, to seize, or to apprehend" an officer of the king. The first English impeachment on record involved a chancellor of Richard II, who was impeached in 1386 simply because he had failed to act as he had promised Parliament he would act. The impeachment precedents Doar and his staff found in English history did not always involve punishment for criminal acts. Impeachment had more often been used as a method of getting at the king's advisers and controlling their activities. Impeachment in English tradition, in short, had been a means to limit the power of the king and cause him to listen to the demands of Parliament and the people.

The committee staff concluded, therefore, that an impeachment of a President could function as a measure designed "primarily to maintain constitutional government." It was a "constitutional safety valve" used to remove a President for charges "based on his entire course of conduct in office." However, the staff memorandum on impeachment concluded, "Not all presidential misconduct is sufficient to constitute grounds for impeachment. There is a further requirement—substantiality." And by substantiality the staff seemed to mean that reasons for impeachment had to be grounded in fact and should not be based on personal opinion or the passion of the moment.

Doar's method of action was to let his staff patiently accumulate data until a case could be made, one way or the other. Chairman Rodino's plan was to allow the committee and staff time enough to consider the issues so that all ramifications of the case had been discussed and taken into account. He wanted no rush to judgment, but most of all, he did not want his committee's final conclusions to be divided along party lines. If the President was to be impeached, it would be the result of a bipartisan effort, with Republicans joining Democrats. And if the President was impeachable, it would take time to win Republicans over to the inevitable decision. Rodino therefore managed the committee so as to maximize the amount of time available to it. To the American public awaiting the outcome of the Judiciary Committee investigation, it seemed as though the committee was taking a painfully long time.

On July 19, 1974, Doar began to summarize the case against Richard Nixon before the members of the Judiciary Committee. The case, said Doar, was a whole pattern of conduct, not a few single, isolated instances of wrongdoing. "I think everyone wants to believe our President. I wanted to believe that he had nothing to do with Watergate." But the evidence, Doar said, proved otherwise. He asked the committee members to read and analyze carefully the more than three hundred pages of summary he handed over to them.

In the days after Doar's summary, the committee members began to feel the need to come to some conclusion. Eighteen of the twenty-one Democrats were known to favor impeachment; ten Republicans still ardently defended the President. That left ten undecided members—three Democrats, all of them from the South, and seven Republicans. Rodino asked Walter Flowers (Democrat, Alabama), one of the undecided members, to discuss the case with others who had come to no final conclusion. Seven of the undecided members met in the office of Tom Railsback and exchanged their opinions. What bothered each of them, they found, was the evidence of Nixon's continued misuse of power. Not any single deed the President had committed convicted him so much as his conception of the power of his office and his willingness to use that power for questionable ends. The seven realized that they were very important to the outcome of the case. If they sided with the majority to impeach, Rodino would have his bipartisan support.

On the evening of July 24, 1974, the House Judiciary Committee began formal sessions before television cameras to consider the impeachment of President Nixon. Chairman Rodino opened the session with a reminder that "this is a turning point, whatever we decide. Our judgment is not concerned with an individual but with a system of constitutional government." Each member was then allowed fifteen minutes to summarize his or her opinions on the case. Robert Kastenmeier (Democrat, Wisconsin) favored impeachment. It was, he said, "the one way in which the American people can say to themselves that they care enough about their institutions, their own freedom and their own claim to self-government, their own national honor, to purge the presidency of anyone who has dishonored that office. Mr. Chairman," he concluded, "in my view Richard Nixon has shown disrespect for the citizens of this nation, and he has violated their Constitution and their laws, engaging in official wrongdoing."

Liberal Kastenmeier's position came as little surprise. But when moderate conservative Tom Railsback's turn to speak arrived, the committee heard its first Republican to condemn the President openly. Railsback listed the misdeeds of the President and his administration, ranging from the abuse of the Internal Revenue Service through Nixon's use of the CIA to stop an investigation of the Watergate affair by the FBI. "Some of my friends from Illinois," Railsback concluded, addressing his constituency, "some of my people say that the country cannot afford to impeach a

President. Let me say to these people . . . I have spoken to countless others including many, many young people, and if the young people in this country think that we are not going to handle this thing fairly, if we are not going to really try to get to the truth, you are going to see the most frustrated people, the most turned-off people, the most disillusioned people . . ." Railsback, in short, wanted impeachment, because it would prove to the young that the American political system worked.

Representative Wiggins, a supporter of the President, spoke for the other side. He asked his colleagues to base their assessment of Nixon's activities purely on law and not on personal opinion. Wiggins believed that "there is not a word, not a word, ladies and gentlemen, of presidential knowledge or awareness or involvement in that wrongful act." He sought to place the blame on Nixon's aides, who had committed the misdeeds.

On Saturday, the first article of impeachment came up for a roll-call vote. The last representative to be given speaking time before the vote was Walter Flowers, who stated, better than anyone else had stated, the exact meaning of the impeachment proceedings. "Make no mistake, my friends," he said, "one of the effects of our action here will be to reduce the influence and the power of the office of the President." Flowers than challenged the House and the Senate to live up to the new responsibility that was being given to them. "In the weeks and months ahead," he concluded, "I want my friends to know that I will be around to remind them when some of these hard choices are up, and we will be able to judge then how responsible we can be with our newly found congressional power."

The first article of impeachment accused the President of obstruction of justice, a felony punishable by imprisonment. It specifically accused Nixon of making false or misleading statements, misusing the CIA, interfering with investigations conducted by the Justice Department, and six other counts of wrongdoing. It passed the committee by a vote of twenty-seven to eleven, with six Republicans and all twenty-one Democrats voting *aye*. Railsback, Cohen, and the other undecided Republicans had cast their votes against the President.

On the following Monday, the committee passed a second article of impeachment by an even larger margin, twenty-eight to ten. This article impeached Nixon for abuse of power while in office and listed six specific instances of abuse of power. They included the authorization of a secret investigative unit "within the office of the President," the failure to see that laws were faithfully executed, and disregard for the rule of law by knowingly misusing executive power to interfere with the CIA, the FBI, and other government agencies.

The third and final article of impeachment was passed on the next day by a vote of twenty-one to seventeen. This article called the President to task for refusing to respond to the subpoenas handed him by the Congress. "In refusing to produce these papers and things, Richard M. Nixon, substituting his judgment as to what materials were necessary for the inquiry, interposed his powers of the Presidency against the lawful subpoenas of the House of Representatives, thereby assuming to himself functions and judgments necessary to the exercise of the sole power of impeachment vested by the Constitution in the House of Representatives."

The Judiciary Committee had completed its work. But the House of Representatives was not to have the opportunity to consider the impeachment of the President. After the Supreme Court had ruled on July 24, 1974—the same day the Judiciary Committee began its final session—that the President had to turn the tapes over to the special prosecutor, Nixon's days as President were numbered. As the information on the tapes became known, even the President's staunchest supporters began to desert him. Representative Charles Wiggins, who had been Nixon's ablest defender on the Judiciary Committee, admitted with sadness that the new information showed that the President was guilty of the charges of which Wiggins had once believed him innocent. Under pressure from Republican leaders in both houses of Congress, Nixon resigned from the presidency on August 9, 1974.

V

THE RESIGNATION of Richard Nixon was the logical outcome of the attempts Congress had been making to gain its rightful place in the American government under the Constitution. When the Watergate affair gained momentum, the House and Senate had for some time been in the midst of a reorganization and reexamination of their practices and powers. Changes had been made to modernize congressional machinery, to open up the activities of Congress to scrutiny by the press and public, and to give every senator and representative a share of authority and influence.

At the same time that these reforms were taking place, there was dissatisfaction among many members of Congress with the secondary role that the House and Senate had assumed over the years and a belief that the executive branch had assumed too many of the powers and prerogatives traditionally exercised by the Congress. Step by step, Congress fought to reacquire these powers by revamping its budgetary system, attacking executive secrecy, challenging the President's authority in foreign affairs and war, and rejecting his nominees to the Supreme Court when they proved inadequate.

It was this Congress that confronted the President on Watergate. The process of investigating Nixon was a slow one. Even in the newly assertive and ambitious Congress, there was great reluctance to take on a President. As the full record of Nixon's misdeeds became known, however, there was little question of the course Congress had to take. If the new Congress, so jealous of its constitutional rights and privileges, had ignored the Watergate affair, it would have been refusing to exercise the very authority under the Constitution that it claimed to want to restore. And if it had refused to take on the President, it would have been succumbing to his power and following the pattern of congressional submission to the imperial presidency.

The Watergate affair, however trivial and sordid it seemed in its particulars, was a major constitutional crisis. In that crisis, one idea of presidential authority was pitted against a theory of government in which the President shared power equally with a legislature and a judiciary. Nixon's use of power, which at times seemed excessive, did not fit into the traditional American concept of governmental power and was rejected. The institutions guaranteed by the Constitution—the free press, the courts, and the Congress—all worked to contribute to his downfall.

CHAPTER TEN

PROBLEMS

Politics is the conduct of public affairs for private advantage—Ambrose Bierce, THE DEVIL'S DICTIONARY

CHANGE HAS been a constant factor in the history of Congress. Since their beginnings in 1789, the House and Senate have frequently altered their practices and procedures to meet new needs and problems. For the most part, these changes have come slowly and have been imperceptible to the public. The period between 1970 and 1976, however, was an exception to this generalization. In a relatively short period of time, Congress altered many customs and traditions that had been accumulating for years.

How has Congress changed? The new Congress is more democratic than previous Congresses. Authority does not rest, as it did a few years ago, on the heads of a few powerful men, but is distributed more widely throughout the membership of the House and Senate. The new Congress is also more open and less secretive than previous Congresses and less likely to accept seniority as the only basis for advancement. Party caucuses have become important instruments for creating and purveying party policy. And finally, the new Congress perceives itself as a branch of government equal to the executive branch and the President in every way.

These are not meager accomplishments and they have done much to make the Congress a more interesting, dynamic, and vital body than it formerly was. Yet there are questions that must be asked about these reforms and about others that were not made. On paper, the congressional changes of recent years sound attractive and completely beneficial; in practice, they have not always proved to be so.

One of the major problems of the new Congress is decentralization. Decentralization of authority has meant that a larger number of senators and representatives now share "a piece of the action," but it also has its more destructive side. It allows individual members of Congress to think of themselves as individuals first and as members of a party or of the Congress second. This means that each senator or representative guards his or her own privileges jealously and may feel reluctant to submit to leadership. This makes for greater democracy and equality of the membership, but at the same time it makes it difficult for Congress to reach a consensus. And without a consensus, legislation cannot be passed.

According to Norman Ornstein, a professor of political science at the Catholic University of America, there is a lack of "followership" in the new Congress. In the old days, he explains, "we had plenty of 'cannon fodder' around—guys who did very little substantively but could always be counted on to back the leaders." Now, senators and representatives want to run things for themselves. The result has been 535 opinions on how things should be done with no agreement on an overall solution.

The failures of decentralization have been many. The Congress, for instance, has been unable to develop a comprehensive energy program to deal with the energy crisis. After President Carter put forth his first standby gas rationing plan, the plan, in spite of strong support from Speaker Thomas O'Neill, was defeated in the House. A point-by-point rebuttal of the plan by Representative David Stockman (Republican, New York) convinced his fellow representatives to vote against it, even though the House offered no alternative plan to help solve the crisis.

The failures of decentralization were brought home another way in 1979 when the House Democratic leadership suffered four significant defeats in one week. The House rejected the plan for the 1980 budget; it refused to adopt a report implementing the Panama Canal treaties; it denied approval of an increase in the federal debt; and it refused to pass a bill raising congressional pay. The four bills were defeated even though Speaker O'Neill could have lost all the Republicans and fifty of his Democrats and still have passed them. Their defeat meant that the House had to spend valuable time drawing up alternative measures to replace the defeated ones.

Thus Congress, in spite of the reforms of the 1970s, still remains organized to deal with narrow problems rather than broad ones. It can pick away at administration bills, but cannot establish a policy of its own. It has no way of ensuring consistency and completeness when it undertakes consideration of the nation's problems. With 435 representatives, 100 senators, and numerous committees and subcommittees in both houses, Congress has too many centers of powers to function coherently and to know its own mind.

Thus decentralization can lead to complete immobilization, with the Congress unable to agree upon the direction in which it should move. Decentralization increases the power of each member of Congress but decreases the power of Congress as a whole. This lack of unity plays into the hands of the President. When Congress fails to act because of divisiveness, it remains for the President to respond. The Congresses during the Great Depression and afterward seemed content to relinquish their powers to the imperial Presidents because they felt inadequate to deal with the problems that faced the nation. The new Congress seems content to preserve its democracy and decentralized powers, even if that means the loss of the ability to act decisively.

Another problem with which the new Congress must deal is the growing power of lobbies and special interest groups. There are now 15,000 lobbyists in Washington, 7,000 more than there were only five years ago. Fewer than 2,000 of them are registered under the lobbying law of the Legislative Reorganization Act of 1946. They spend more than $1 billion a year to influence opinion in Washington and an additional $1 billion a year to orchestrate public opinion throughout the country.

Indeed, the lobbyists have become so powerful that they were able in 1978 to destroy a bill that would have required them to reveal the sources of their money, the people and interests they represent, and the legislation they seek to shape. The bill passed the House of Representatives but died in the Senate Governmental Affairs Committee, in spite of the support of the committee's chairman, Abraham Ribicoff (Democrat, Connecticut).

The failure of the bill led Ribicoff to warn, "Lobbying has reached a new dimension and is more effective than ever in history. It has become a big computerized operation in which the Congress and the public are being bombarded by single-issue groups. The Congress and the public should be aware of who's trying to influence whom and why and what for." The bill's failure likewise led two prominent senators and a representative to sign a joint statement that read, "Without lobbying, government could not function. The flow of information to Congress and to every federal agency is a vital part of our democratic system." But, they concluded, "There is a darker side to lobbying. It derives from the secrecy of lobbying and the widespread suspicion, even when totally unjustified, that secrecy breeds undue influence and corruption."

How do lobbyists work in the age of the computer? One of

the most powerful lobbies in Washington is the Chamber of Commerce. Four of its lobbyists in Congress watch the development of every bill that is of concern to businessmen and send out an alert when an important legislative action is approaching. The word goes quickly to 1,200 local congressional action committees with some 100,000 members. Through the various publications of the Chamber of Commerce, the alert reaches seven million people. When the Washington headquarters of the Chamber of Commerce declares an "action call," the members of Congress are besieged with mail attacking or supporting the proposed bill.

The Chamber of Commerce also has six regional offices in which fifty professionals keep track of the interests and concerns of senators and representatives in their area. These professionals look for and find friends and others who have influence on these senators and representatives. At critical times, the friends and associates of the senators and representatives are called upon to influence the members of Congress to vote one way or another on the legislation under consideration.

In recent years, lobbies have destroyed President Carter's plan for a consumer protection agency and have killed strip mining laws opposed by the coal companies. They have sought and received special provisions that exempt big irrigators in the West from acreage limitations on their ranches and that relieved asbestos producers from sharing the costs of removing their cancer-causing insulation from school walls. They have affected legislation involving oil, tourism, shipyards, steel, and innumerable other areas of importance to the country.

Outspoken Representative Millicent Fenwick (Republican, New Jersey) has frequently criticized her colleagues for their quick and easy acceptance of lobbyists. "In my mind," she has said, "there is a connection" between the contributions lobbyists offer and the way a member of Congress votes. "I have sought votes, and members have told me they received such and such an amount of money from one of these groups and they could not vote with me."

No doubt the Congress will address the problems of decentralization and lobbying. But the question is when? Already, these two problems have undermined some of the spirit of the reforms of the 1970s and have created a fragmented, divided Congress that seems less inclined to consider the public good than to rush to the aid of the special interests. But Congress is an ever-changing institution and what seems pressing at one moment may not seem important later on. Perhaps the final comment should be that of Representative George Mahon (Democrat, Texas). What Congress needs, Mahon said during the reforms of the 1970s, is not more "reform of procedures and methods, we need more reform of the will."

SUGGESTIONS FOR FURTHER READING

An asterisk (*) denotes a book of special interest to younger readers.

General Background. No student of American government and politics should fail to read Alexander Hamilton, James Madison, and John Jay, *The Federalist Papers* * (New York: New American Library, 1961). The three authors wrote these "papers" or essays after the Constitutional Convention to defend the new Constitution and urge its acceptance by the original thirteen states. Alexis de Tocqueville, *Democracy in America* * (New York: Schocken Books, 1967), first published in 1835 and 1840, is one of the best books ever written on the American political system. There are many good general histories of the United States, but one of the most helpful is Samuel Eliot Morison, *The Oxford History of the American People* * (New York: Oxford University Press, 1965).

On the background and proceedings of the Constitutional Convention, see Clinton Rossiter, *1787: The Grand Convention* (New York: Macmillan, 1966) and Charles Warren, *The Making of the Constitution* (Boston: Little, Brown, 1928). On how the Congress has worked in practice, see Ernest Sutherland Bates, *The Story of Congress 1789–1935* * (New York: Harper & Brothers, 1936) and Alvin Josephy, Jr., *The American Heritage History of the Congress of the United States* * (New York: American Heritage Publishing Co., 1975).

Several important works on the recent history of Congress are Daniel Berman, *In Congress Assembled* * (New York: Macmillan, 1964); Stephen Bailey, *The New Congress* (New York: St. Martin's Press, 1966); Robert Bendiner, *Obstacle Course on Capitol Hill* * (New York: McGraw-Hill, 1964); Samuel Patterson, *The Legislative Process in the United States* (New York: Random House, 1973); and Lawrence Dodd and Bruce Oppenheimer, editors, *Congress Reconsidered* (New York: Praeger, 1977).

Congressional Quarterly, Inc., a private editorial research service and publishing company in Washington, D.C., puts out the *Congressional Quarterly Weekly Report*, an extremely helpful guide to the Congress. Congressional Quarterly also publishes many useful books, including *Origins and Development of Congress* * (1976) and *Powers of Congress* (1976). These books contain a wealth of information and are compiled by the staff of Congressional Quarterly.

The *Congressional Record* (Washington, D.C.: U. S. Government Printing Office) is the complete record of the proceedings of the House of Representatives and the Senate. The reader is warned, however, that representatives and senators are allowed to alter statements they have made in the House or Senate before the *Record* is published and to insert information that was not read in Congress. The *Congressional Record*, therefore, is not an accurate guide to the day-to-day proceedings of Congress and should be used with care. The *Congressional Directory* (Washington, D.C.: U.S. Government Printing Office) is published regularly and gives a biographical profile of every member of Congress as well as other useful information.

James Hamilton, *The Power to Probe; A Study of Congressional Investigations* * (New York: Random House, 1976) offers an analysis of the investigations Congress has conducted over the years. Harrison Fox, Jr., and Susan Webb, *Congressional Staffs; The Invisible Force in Lawmaking* (New York: The Free Press, 1977) looks into the work of the aides and assistants of representatives and senators. Bill Severn, *Democracy's Messengers; The Capitol Pages* * (New York: Hawthorn Books, 1975) discusses the work of the young men and women who serve as pages on Capitol Hill.

Woodrow Wilson, *Congressional Government* (Magnolia, Mass.: Peter Smith, 1973) is a classic study of the problems faced by Congress near the end of the nineteenth century written by a man who later became President of the United States. Congressional corruption and other misdeeds of senators and representatives are the subject of Drew Pearson and Jack Anderson, *The Case Against Congress* * (New York: Simon & Schuster, 1968) and David Zwick, *Who Runs Congress?* * (New York: Bantam, 1972). The Zwick book is a report of the Ralph Nader Congress Project.

The House of Representatives. Neil MacNeil, *Forge of Democracy: The House of Representatives* * (New York: David McKay, 1963) is a lively, interesting, and generally favorable study of the House. A more scholarly book is George Galloway, *History of the House of Representatives* (New York: Thomas Y. Crowell, 1976). For a look at the committee system of the House and the nature of House leadership, see Mary P. Follett, *The Speaker of the House of Representatives* (New York: Burt Franklin Reprints, 1974); Richard Fenno, *The Power of the Purse; Appropriations Politics in Congress* (Boston: Little, Brown, 1966); and James Robinson, *The House Rules Committee* (New York: Bobbs-

Merrill, 1963). Roger Davidson and Walter Oleszek, *Congress Against Itself* (Bloomington, Ind.: Indiana University Press, 1977) is a detailed analysis of some of the attempts at congressional reform in the 1970s.

Anyone interested in the House should take a look at Asher C. Hinds, *Precedents of the House of Representatives* (Washington, D.C.: U.S. Government Printing Office, 1907). A glance at this work—it is eight volumes long—will give the reader an idea of the complexity of House procedures. Champ Clark, *My Quarter Century of American Politics* * (New York: Harper, 1920) is the memoirs of a former Democratic leader in the House from Missouri. Richard Bolling, a prominent current member of the House, likewise a Democrat from Missouri, discusses the problems of the House in *House Out of Order* * (New York: Dutton, 1965) and *Power in the House* * (New York: Dutton, 1968).

The Senate. Two important works on the Senate are George Haynes, *The Senate of the United States; Its History and Practice* (Boston: Houghton Mifflin, 1938) and Joseph Harris, *The Advice and Consent of the Senate* (Westport, Conn.: Greenwood Press, 1968). The Harris book is a study of the role the Senate plays in the confirmation of presidential appointments. Franklin Burdette, *Filibustering in the Senate* * (New York: Russell & Russell, 1965) takes a look at the Senate's use of its right of unlimited speech.

Individual senators have frequently published memoirs or commentaries on the Senate that are well worth reading. In this category are Thomas Hart Benton, *Thirty Years' View* * (Westport, Conn.: Greenwood Press, 1968); Joseph Clark, *Congress: The Sapless Branch* * (New York: Harper & Row, 1964) and *The Senate Establishment* * (New York: Hill and Wang, 1963); and James L. Buckley, *If Men Were Angels* * (New York: G. P. Putnam's, 1975). Bernard Asbell, *The Senate Nobody Knows* * (New York: Doubleday & Company, 1978) looks at the Senate through the eyes of Senator Edmund Muskie of Maine. Elizabeth Drew, *Senator* * (New York: Simon & Schuster, 1979) is a thorough description of several working days in the life of Senator John Culver of Iowa. Frank Madison, *A View from the Floor; The Journal of a United States Senate Page Boy* * (Englewood Cliffs, N.J.: Prentice-Hall, 1967) is a description of the day-to-day activities of a Senate page by a man who once served as a page.

Other Books of Interest. Arthur Schlesinger, Jr., *The Imperial Presidency* (Boston: Houghton Mifflin, 1973) is the best summary of the expansion of presidential power during the administration of Franklin Roosevelt and afterward. Elizabeth Drew, *Washington Journal: The Events of 1973–74* * (New York: Random House, 1975) and *American Journal: The Events of 1976* * (New York: Random House, 1977) offer a wealth of information and wisdom about recent politics. Ms. Drew is one of the best observers of Washington life. For a summary of the Watergate Affair, see Theodore White, *Breach of Faith: The Fall of Richard Nixon* * (New York: Reader's Digest Press, 1975).

INDEX

Adams, John, 33-34, 47, 49, 65, 83
Albert, Carl, 139-40, 145
Aldrich, Nelson, 86
Allison, William, 85-86
Amendments to the Constitution (Bill of Rights), 47
  See also specific amendments
Anthony Rule, 90
Appropriations, 40, 80-81
  See also Budget, federal
Appropriations Committee of the House, 70, 71, 80
Appropriations Committee of the Senate, 80-81
Aristocracy, 33-35
Army, Department of the, 132-34
Army, power to raise and support an, 42
Articles of Confederation, 32-33

Baker, Bobby, 134-35
Banking and Currency Committee, 70
Bank of the United States, 77-78
Bayh, Birch, 180
Benton, Thomas Hart, 22-23, 63, 75-76
Beveridge, Albert, 88
Bill of Rights (Amendments to the Constitution), 47
Bills of attainder, 47
Blaine, James G., 53, 85
Bolling committee (House Select Committee on Committees), 152-53
Borrow, power to, 40
Bricker amendment, 175

Bryce, James, 76
Budget, federal, 165-70
Budget Act of 1974, 168-70
Budget committees, 168-69
Burdette, Franklin, 90
Butler, Pierce, 42
Butterfield, Alexander, 187, 189

Calendar Wednesday, 56-57
Calhoun, John C., 15, 92
Cambodia, invasion of, 113, 176
Campaign contributions and expenditures, 152
Campbell, Philip, 67
Cannon, Joseph, 24, 26, 55-59, 60
Carlisle, John, 53
Carswell, G. Harrold, 180-81
Case, Clifford, 138, 176
Caucuses, 59
  of Democratic party, 145-46, 148, 149, 154, 155
Central Intelligence Agency (CIA), 174-75
Chamber of Commerce, 204
Checks and balances, system of, 48-49
China, 103
Chiu, Chang-wei, 67
Church, Frank, 115, 176
Civil rights, 16-17, 26, 128, 129
Clay, Henry, 15, 23, 52-53, 69, 77-79, 89
Closed rules, 100
Cloture rule, 92, 129-30, 161
Codes of conduct (or ethics), 137-38, 140, 151-52
Cold war, 104, 107, 108
Colmer, William, 127
Commerce, powers to regulate, 11-12, 40-42
Committee of the Whole House, 62-63
Committee on Committees, Democratic, 146-47
Committee on Committees, House Select (Bolling committee), 152-53
Committees of the House of Representatives, 53, 67-73
  chairmen of, 58-60, 122, 154-56
  decentralization of power and, 71, 73
  expenditures and, 69-71
  investigations by, 68-69
  reform of, 123, 143-44, 146-48, 150, 153-56
  secrecy of, 71-72
  select, 62, 68
  seniority system and, 72
  standards of behavior, 133
  standing, 62, 68
  See also Subcommittees of the House of Representatives; *and specific committees*
Committees of the Senate, 92-96, 122
  openness rules and, 160
  reform of, 123, 143-44, 159-61
Congressional Budget Office (CBO), 168-69

Conkling, Roscoe, 84
Constitutional Convention (1787), 31-49
Corruption and dishonesty, 17-21
Corwin, Edwin, 105
Coudert, Frederic, Jr., 105
Cox, Archibald, 190

Dalzell, John, 57-58
Dawes, Oakes, 17-18
Dean, John, 186-87
Decentralization, 71, 73, 149, 201-3
Democratic Committee on Committees, 145-47
Democratic party caucus, 145-46, 148, 149, 154, 155
Democratic Steering and Policy Committee, 147-49, 155-56
Democratic Study Group (DSG), 145
De Tocqueville, Alexis, 9, 76
Dickinson, John, 38
Diggs, Charles, 152
Doar, John, 192-94
Dodd, Thomas, 135
Dominican Republic, invasion of (1965), 109-10
Douglas, Paul, 104-5

Ehrlichman, John, 186, 187
Eisenhower, Dwight D., 106-8, 132
Ellsberg, Daniel, 118-19, 173
Emergency powers, *see* War powers
English Parliament, 50, 76
Ervin, Sam, 111, 116, 117, 119, 184-88
Ethics, codes of, 137-38, 140, 151-52
Executive branch, *see* President (presidency)
Executive privilege, doctrine of, 106-7, 119
  Watergate affair and, 188-90
Ex post facto laws, 47

Faulkner, C. J., 89
Federal Bureau of Investigation, 174-75
Filibustering, 63, 161
  in the Senate, 88-92, 128-30
First Amendment, 47
Florence, William, 172
Flowers, Walter, 194, 196
Follett, Mary Parker, 71
Foote, Henry "Hangman," 22
Ford, Gerald, 178
Foreign policy, 12, 45, 175
  bipartisan, 104
Franklin, Benjamin, 49
Fulbright, William, 108

Gardener, Barent, 63
Garner, John Nance, 23
Gesell, Gerhard, 189-90
Gladstone, William, 76
Great Depression, 99
Gruening, Ernest, 16, 17

Habeas corpus, writ of, 47

Halleck, Charles, 126, 127
Hamilton, Alexander, 31
Hanna, Mark, 84
Hansen, Julia Butler, 146
Hansen committee (Committee on Organization, Study, and Review), 146-49
Haynsworth, Clement, Jr., 179-80
Hays, Wayne, 18, 19, 154
Hinds, Asher, 64
House of Representatives, 50-73
  Code of Official Conduct of, 137
  committees of, *see* Committees of the House of Representatives
  increased workloads of, 50-51
  oversight subcommittees, 152
  radio and television coverage of, 132-33, 150-51
  reform of
    Bolling committee reform, 153
    code of ethics, 137, 140, 151-52
    committee system, 123 143-44, 146-48, 150, 153-56
    Hansen committee reforms (1971-1974), 146-49
    1973-1975 reforms, 149, 150
    openness rules, 150, 162
    party government, 155-56
    radio and television coverage, 150-51
    Rules Committee, 66-67, 125-28, 156
    Speaker of the House and, 147-49, 156
    subcommittee system, 146-49, 154, 162-63
    See also Reform of Congress
  Franklin Roosevelt and, 100-1
  rules and customs of, 24, 38, 60-67
  the Senate compared to, 74-76, 87
  Senate's relationship to, 78-81
  Speaker of the, 51-60, 66, 73, 139-40, 147-49, 156
  subcommittees of, 146-49, 152, 154
  See also Representatives
Humphrey, Hubert, 15-17, 130

Impeachment, 46
  of Nixon, 191-98
Imperial presidency, 98-99, 102-3, 111-12, 175
Impoundment of funds, 116, 167-68, 170
Income tax, 40
Ingalls, John, 87
Investigations, Congressional, 13, 68-69

Jackson, Andrew, 22*n*, 69, 77-78, 89
Javits, Jacob, 177

Jaworski, Leon, 191
Jefferson, Thomas, 65*n*, 87
Johnson, Andrew, 46, 79
Johnson, Lyndon, 108-11, 114, 129-30, 140
Joint Committee on Congressional Operations, 144, 145
Joint Committee on the Organization of Congress, 122-23
Joint Study Committee on Budget Control, 167, 168
Judges, Presidential power to appoint, 45
Judiciary, 34, 45-46
Judiciary Committee of the House: Watergate affair and, 151, 191-98

Kansas-Nebraska bill (1854), 64, 65
Kastenmeier, Robert, 195
Kennedy, John, 108, 126
Korean War, 104

La Follette, Robert, 15, 90-91
La Follette, Robert, Jr., 122-23
Legislative Reorganization Act of 1946, 123-24, 167
Legislative Reorganization Act of 1970, 143-45, 160
Lincoln, Abraham, 16, 79, 114
Lippmann, Walter, 119
Lobbyists, 14, 124, 149-50, 203-4
Lodge, Henry Cabot, 90

McCarthy, Joseph, 131-34
McCormack, John, 139, 145
Madison, James, 10, 23, 48-49, 69, 171
  at Constitutional Convention, 31, 33, 34, 36, 37
Mansfield, Mike, 140, 176, 184-85
Marshall, John, 41
Media
  coverage of House activities by radio and television, 132-33, 150-51
  Nixon and, 116-17
  the President and, 98
Mencken, H. L., 20-21
Militia, 42-43
Mills, Wilbur, 18-19, 154
Mollenhoff, Clark, 107
Monroney, Mike, 123, 143
Morris, Gouverneur, 44, 48
Morse, Wayne, 16, 17
Muhlenberg, Frederick, 60

Nelson, John, 56
Nixon, Richard M., 111-20, 129, 176, 177
  Congress and, 115-16
  impoundment of funds by, 116, 167-68
  intelligence activities and, 118-19
  media and, 116-17
  resignation of, 13, 30, 46, 79, 198
  secrecy system and, 172-74

Nixon, Richard M. (*contd.*)
Supreme Court appointments by, 12-13, 179-82
war powers of, 113-14
Watergate affair and, 119, 186-98
White House staff and assistants of, 112-13
Norris, George, 57

Omnibus bill plan, 167
Oppenheimer, Bruce, 156

Parliament, English, 50, 76
Party caucuses, 59
Democratic, 145-46, 148, 149, 154, 155
Patman, Wright, 154-55, 184
Pentagon papers case, 117-19, 173-74
Permanent Investigations Subcommittee of the Senate, 131-32, 134
Philosophy Club, 85
Pinckney, Charles, 46
"Plumbers, the," 118-19
Pork barrel schemes, 70
Powell, Adam Clayton, 135-37
Powers of Congress, 11-13, 39-43
President, the (presidency)
imperial, 98-99, 102-3, 111-12, 175
media coverage of, 98
powers and authority of, 28-30, 97-99, 164
war powers, 42, 176-78
relationship between Congress and, 163-65
budget-making process, 165-70
Constitutional Convention and, 44, 46, 48
under Eisenhower, 106-8
foreign affairs and, 175-76, 178
under Johnson, 109-11
under Nixon, 115-16
under Franklin Roosevelt, 99-103
secrecy and, 170-75
under Truman, 103-5
war-making powers, 176-78
the Senate and, 77-79
veto power of, 45
war powers of, *see* War powers
See also individual presidents
Presidential appointments, 45-46
right to confirm or dismiss, 12-13
to the Supreme Court, 178-82
President pro tempore of the Senate, 84, 93
Privileges and Elections Committee, 82
Public interest lobbies, 149-50
Purse, power of the, 11, 39-40

Quay, Matthew, 85
Quorum, disappearing, 54-55

Radio, *see* Media
Railsback, Tom, 192, 194-97

Randall, Samuel, 65-66, 70, 71
Randolph, Edmund, 74
Randolph, John, 22, 63, 64*n*
Rayburn, Sam, 42, 107-8, 125-27, 132-33, 139
Reed, Thomas B., 16, 53-55
Reedy, George, 109
Reform of Congress, 26-28, 30, 121-63
 cloture rule, 128-30
 committee system, 123-24
 Hansen committee and, 146-49
 Legislative Reorganization Act of 1946, 123-24
 Legislative Reorganization Act of 1970, 143-45
 personal conduct and use of power, 130-38
 See also House of Representatives—reform of
Rehnquist, William, 114, 116
Representatives
 changes in characteristics of, 139
 election of, 35
 number of, 23-24, 36, 51, 63*n*
 qualifications of, 37-38
 term of, 37
Republican conference of the House, 146-48
Rodino, Peter, 191, 192, 194, 195
Rogers, Will, 20, 21
Roosevelt, Franklin, 79, 99-103
Rules and customs of the House of Representatives, 24, 38, 60-67
 Franklin Roosevelt and, 100-1
Rules and customs of the Senate, 24, 38, 87-92, 128-30
 cloture rule, 92, 128-30, 161
Rules Committee of the House, 56-60, 133
 functions of, 156-58
 reforms of, 66-67, 125-28, 156
 Franklin Roosevelt and, 100-1

Scandals involving Congressmen, 17-19, 134-37
Schlesinger, Arthur, Jr., 98, 115, 171
Secrecy system, 170-75
Select committees, 62, 68
Senate, the, 74-96
 as aristocratic and elitist, 36, 48-49
 code of conduct of, 137-38, 140
 committees of, 92-96
 debate in, 75
 filibustering in, 88-92, 128-30, 161
 House of Representatives compared to, 74-76, 87
 House of Representatives' relationship to, 79-81
 leadership of, 83-86, 140
 the President and, 77-79
 reform of the 1970s in, 158-63
  See also Reform of Congress
 Franklin Roosevelt and, 101
 rules and customs of, 24, 38, 87-92, 128-30, 161
 secrecy system and, 173, 174

Senate, the (*contd.*)
seniority system in, 159-60
states and state legislatures and, 81-83
Watergate affair and, 184-90
Senators
changes in characteristics of, 139
election of, 26, 36, 82-83
number of, 23, 24, 36-37
qualifications of, 37-38
term of, 37
Seniority system, 25, 144, 162
in the House, 72, 122, 146, 147, 155
in the Senate, 94, 122, 159-60
Seventeenth Amendment, 26, 82-83
Sherman, Roger, 34, 35, 37, 42, 44
Sirica, John J., 189
Slavery, 64, 65
Smith, Howard W., 126, 127
Smith, Margaret Chase, 15-17
Speaker of the House, 51-60, 66, 73, 139-40, 156
reforms of the 1970s and, 147-49
See also individual speakers
Standards and Conduct, Senate Select Committee on, 134, 137-38
Standards of Official Conduct, House Committee on, 137, 152
Standing committees
of the House of Representatives, 68
of the Senate, 92-95
State legislatures, the Senate and, 81-83
Steel mills, nationalization of (1952), 105
Steering and Policy Committee, Democratic, 147-49, 155-56
Subcommittees of the House of Representatives, 146-49, 154
oversight, 152
Sumner, Charles, 23
Supreme Court, Presidential appointments to, 178-82
"Sweeping clause," 43

Taft, Robert, 15, 105, 172
Taxation, power of, 39-40
Taylor, Telford, 107
Television, *see* Media
Tillman, Benjamin "Pitchfork Ben," 90, 91
Tonkin Gulf Resolution, 110-11, 176
Treaties, power to ratify or reject, 12
Truman, Harry, 103-6
Twain, Mark, 19-20
21-day rule, 125-27
Tydings, Millard, 133
Tyler, John, 78-79

Un-American Activities Committee, House, 131-33
Unanimous consent calendar, 56

Values of the American people, Congress as reflecting, 14-15
Veto power of the President, 45
Vice-President, as president of the Senate, 83
Vietnam War, 13, 17, 110-11, 113, 176
Voorhis, Jerry, 121, 122

War powers, 42
  of Eisenhower, 107-8
  of Johnson, 109-11
  under Lincoln, 114
  under Nixon, 113-14
  restrictions on, 176-78
  of Roosevelt, 101-2
  of Truman, 104-5
War Powers Act of 1973, 176-78
Watergate affair, 119, 151, 183-99
  executive privilege and, 188-90
  House Judiciary Committee and, 191-98
  Senate and, 184-90
Ways and Means Committee, 68, 70, 147, 148
Webster, Daniel, 15
Wiggins, Charles, 191-92, 196-98
Wilson, James, 34-36, 38
Wilson, Woodrow, 12, 59, 71, 75, 79, 91-92
World War II, 101-2

ABOUT THE AUTHOR

STEPHEN GOODE was born in Elkins, West Virginia. He holds a B.A. from Davison College, an M.A. from the University of Virginia, a Ph. D. from Rutgers University, and has studied in Vienna and Budapest. Mr. Goode was a lecturer in history at Rutgers University. For the last seven years he has lived in Washington, D.C., where he pursues his interest in government and politics. He is the author of a number of books in these fields, including *Affluent Revolutionaries, Guerrilla Warfare and Terrorism,* and *Assassination: Kennedy, King, Kennedy.*